PRAISE FOR
DECISIONAL PREACHING

Biblical preaching should move hearers to respond. In *Decisional Preaching*, Jim Shaddix shows us how to do just that. Drawing from his decades of experience behind the pulpit, Shaddix provides a much-needed manual for applying this principle to our own preaching. If you want your preaching to be clear, impactful, and challenging, you need to read this book.

Robby Gallaty, Pastor
Longhollow Baptist Church

Preachers should preach for a response. When Jesus, Paul and Peter preached, they expected their listeners to respond then and there. No one should seek "easy believism." But the Gospel does demand a response and those who preach the Gospel must call for it. In his new book, *Decisional Preaching*, Dr. Jim Shaddix explains why we should call for a response when we preach, and also how to do it. This is a timely book that I highly recommend.

Steve Gaines, Pastor
Pastor, Bellevue Baptist Church, Memphis, TN

There is a famine in too much of today's preaching when it comes to calling people to decide for Christ. You can believe in biblical decisional preaching without believing in unbiblical decisional regeneration. Jim Shaddix makes this abundantly clear in a compelling manner in this work. Strengthen your preaching by mining the wealth of truth in this book.

Daniel L. Akin, President
Southeastern Baptist Theological Seminary

Preaching necessarily involves persuading people to repent and believe the gospel. My mentor in preaching, Jim Shaddix, not only shows how this is biblically true, but also provides practical, pastoral instruction for bringing people to decision every time we preach God's Word. I wholeheartedly recommend this helpful book.

David Platt, Pastor
Maclean Bible Church

Preachers, you just lost your reason to avoid exploring the role of persuasion in the pulpit ministry of a pastor. *Decisional Preaching* by Jim Shaddix is biblical, theological, philosophical, functional, and transferrable. You are unlikely to find another work on this subject as comprehensive and as concise, as informative and as interesting as this book. It will be in the hands of students in seminary classrooms and pastors in search of pulpit excellence. It is too thorough for professors to overlook and too interesting for pastors getting ready for Sunday to ignore."

Chuck Kelley, President
New Orleans Baptist Theological Seminary

Jim Shaddix is one of my favorite preachers. He is also one of my favorite homileticians. *Decisional Preaching* is a much-needed book on an oft-neglected subject. Clear, concise, biblical, and practical, this book answers the question of the what and the why of preaching for a verdict! Offer and persuade—this is the responsibility of every preacher! I wish I could place this book in the hands of every preacher. Highly recommended!

David Allen, Dean
School of Preaching
Southwestern Baptist Theological Seminary

Whatever Jim Shaddix writes on preaching is worth reading—especially by those who are called to preach. In Decisional Preaching, Shaddix advances the dialog on preaching for a verdict, and in so doing raises a host of issues worth reflecting on and applying to one's pulpit ministry. I'm grateful to God for Jim Shaddix and for this book he's so capably written.

Jason K. Allen, Ph.D.
President
Midwestern Baptist Theological Seminary & Spurgeon College

DECISIONAL PREACHING

Jim Shaddix

Decisional Preaching
© 2019 by Jim Shaddix
All rights reserved.

ISBN 978-1-948022-12-5

Rainer Publishing
www.RainerPublishing.com
Spring Hill, TN

Printed in the United States of America

Scripture quotations are from the ESV® Bible (The Holy Bible, English Standard Version®), copyright © 2001 by Crossway, a publishing ministry of Good News Publishers. Used by permission. All rights reserved.

*To Chuck Kelley and Richard Jackson,
who helped me think better about calling for a verdict when I preach,
both evangelistically and pastorally.*

CONTENTS

Introduction - "Nobody Oozes into the Kingdom of God" 11
Chapter I - Confessions ofa Spurgeonist 19
Chapter II - Preparing to Call for Decisions 39
Chapter III - Decisional Qualities of Sermon Foundation 59
Chapter IV - Decisional Qualities of Sermon Function 77
Chapter V - Decisional Qualities of Sermon Force 99
Chapter VI - Public Expressions of Spiritual Decisions 119
Conclusion - "We Persuade Men" 135

INTRODUCTION

"NOBODY OOZES INTO THE KINGDOM OF GOD"

That's what my mentor, Dr. Roy Fish, professor of evangelism at Southwestern Seminary, taught me way back in the mid-1980s. He would say, "One does not become a Christian by osmosis. Nobody oozes into the kingdom of God."[1] While he spoke in terms of how he believed people are saved, his major concern was what we need to do when we're sharing the Gospel with people. He believed we are responsible for offering everyone an opportunity to confess Christ and for compelling them to do so.

I honestly don't know if Dr. Fish and I would agree on every aspect of how the new birth comes about in a person's soul. I'm a little bit embarrassed to say that I don't think we ever had that conversation, or at least I don't remember it if we did. But I do think that what he believed about personal evangelism is true for preaching. Preachers are responsible for offering everyone an opportunity to decide rightly for the truth we preach, and for persuading them to do so. I think that's true whether we're calling unbelievers to repent and be justified or whether we're calling believers to repent and be sanctified. While "nobody oozes into the kingdom of God," neither does anyone ooze into obedience. To be sure, Christlikeness is a process, but obedience that leads to Christlikeness is a decision.

I'm indebted to one of my other mentors, Chuck Kelley, president of New Orleans Seminary, for helping me to think through the important role of calling for a decision in Christian preaching. I was introduced to the term *decisional preaching* through his book *How Did They Do It?* (Insight, 1993), a historical account of evangelism in my denomination, the Southern Baptist Convention. The book recently has been revised, updated and re-released under the title *Fuel the Fire: Lessons from the History of Southern Baptist Evangelism* (B&H, 2018). In his work Kelley defines decisional preaching as preaching "that draws a 'line in the sand' about a person's relationship with God. It's purpose is to bring the hearer to a point of decision about how to respond to God's dealing with his or her soul." [2]

Kelley goes on to show how Southern Baptist homileticians fostered persuasion in Gospel preaching by teaching preaching students to prepare and deliver sermons with a view toward calling for decision. He observes:

> Invention, arrangement, style, delivery, and memory became the organizational framework for teaching students how to preach. From the beginning, Southern Baptists were taught to link biblical proclamation with rhetorical intent. Preachers must proclaim the word of God with a view to persuading men and women to respond to God's call for repentance, faith, and obedience.[3]

Our preachers have been taught that calling for a decision is a logical result of the rhetorical emphasis on homiletical theory. So most of us Southern Baptist preachers have grown up with a bent toward calling on people to decide something about the message. We believe the sermon does more than make the Gospel known. It makes the *demands* of the Gospel known and calls for a response. So, "the purpose of preaching is to persuade the will as well as to inform the mind."[4]

One of the primary purposes of preaching, then, is to persuade the will as well as to inform the mind. Jason Allen rightly observes, "Preaching is to inform the mind, impact the emotion, and challenge the will. Real preaching is confrontational, always calling for a verdict, and that should happen throughout the sermon, not just during the conclusion."[5] Christian preaching aims at seeing people choose regarding its message, either to accept it or reject it. Our prayer, of course, is that they would always choose rightly regarding God's truth.

I would contend, however, that when it comes to decision-making, Christian preaching brings another element to the table—the Gospel of Christ presented in the power of the Spirit. And it's this element that fosters decisions that are more than mere intellectual resolutions. Speaking about his preaching ministry in Corinth, the Apostle Paul says,

> And I, when I came to you, brothers, did not come proclaiming to you the testimony of God with lofty speech or wisdom. For I decided to know nothing among you except Jesus Christ and him crucified. And I was with you in weakness and in fear and much trembling, and my speech and my message were not in plausible words of wisdom, but in demonstration of the Spirit and of power, so that your faith might not rest in the wisdom of men but in the power of God. (1 Cor 2:1–5)

Paul is speaking of the kind of decision-making that reflects supernatural life change through faith in God. This is one of the qualities that distinguishes preaching and its decisional goal from the persuasive speech that characterizes a salesperson, politician, news commentator, actor or actress, and all other public communicators who are trying to convince people of something.

Preaching involves the other-worldly act of leading people to say "yes" to the Gospel of Christ, to decide rightly about it and all of its implications for the crucified life. Paul asserted that his goal was for his listeners to decide to put their faith in God's power instead of man's wisdom. And, he proposed, such faith was brought about by the message of "Jesus Christ and him crucified" (1 Cor 2:2) and the "demonstration of the Spirit and of power" (1 Cor. 2:4). Christian preaching is aimed at a decision, a faith decision to trust God for life change, a faith decision to depend on Him to do something we can't do for ourselves. And what makes that possible is the work of the Gospel as it's carried along by the effectual work of the Holy Spirit.

My exposure to this understanding of preaching for a verdict led me to dedicate my Ph.D. dissertation to the subject. In the course of my study I identified a pastor named Richard Jackson who seemed to exemplify a potent decisional quality in his pastoral preaching. Jackson pastored the North Phoenix Baptist Church in Phoenix, Arizona, for over twenty years. During the decade of the 1980s, North Phoenix led the Southern Baptist Convention in baptisms seven out of ten years. That statistic was especially fascinating to me because Arizona isn't exactly the Bible Belt! Still today it's considered a "new work" or "pioneer" area by most North American missiological standards.

I was fully aware that responses to the preached Word weren't limited to the salvation experience or to subsequent baptism. Years ago the great preaching professor V. L. Stanfield identified one possible response for unbelievers (receiving Christ as Lord and Savior) and five possible responses for believers (rededication, transfer of membership, baptism, vocational service, and commitment to some specific area of Christian living).[6] While I might use some different categories, I think he was right in proposing that preaching calls for a variety of spiritual decisions, ranging from an initial confession of Christ to living out every aspect of the crucified life determined by that confession. Although the baptism numbers at North Phoenix during that ten-year period primarily represented conversions, in my estimation they were indicative of a variety of spiritual decisions made through the church's ministry.

I also was confident that, while many factors certainly contributed to the multitude of spiritual decisions during those years, the centrality of the preaching event in the church's corporate worship services at the very least implied that Jackson's preaching played a key role in fostering them. On one occasion, as he was expounding Acts 26:27, he even provided a summary of his own philosophy and practice of preaching. As he was pressing for a decision from his listeners, he explained,

> Paul is pressing for a decision. Calling Agrippa, and not the excited Festus by name, he states, "Why, of course you do. A man of your expertise in matters Hebraic could hardly learn so much without being convinced." He tackles Agrippa head-on. He makes Agrippa responsible. Once one has heard the Gospel and the Holy Spirit comes to prompt that heart to believe, we become responsible because we know the truth.[7]

Jackson wasn't shy about confronting his listeners. Once people heard the truth, he held them responsible to act on it.

So I decided to analyze Richard Jackson's sermons during that decade to see if I could identify elements that contributed to the call for various spiritual decisions. I first surveyed preaching books throughout church history to see what factors were associated with the call for decision. Then I developed a lens from those findings through which I scrutinized Jackson's messages. The results of that analysis, along with over thirty-five years of additional research and personal preaching experience—as well as the apparent famine of decisional preaching in our day—together have inspired me to write this book.

One of the burdens I bring to this project is that—even in my own camp—there is a diversity of opinions and practices when it comes to this subject. I'm fully aware that Southern Baptist preachers aren't the only ones who historically have called for a verdict when we preach God's truth. Many of you who aren't Southern Baptist share this same conviction. But if the decline in baptisms in my denomination in any way reflects on decisional preaching, then even our group isn't doing a very good job of it anymore. While I know there are other factors that contribute to such a trend, certainly what we're doing—or not doing— in the pulpit is playing some role. We have more churches but fewer baptisms. More sermons are being preached, but fewer decisions are being made—at least decisions for Christ. You can do the math. There's so much preaching today that announces the glorious truths of the Gospel but never ever compels anyone to decide for them.

Throughout my own personal journey, I've become more and more convinced of three facts that I believe are true for all of us who preach. First, there's a relationship between certain sermonic elements and a decisional emphasis in the preaching event. Not all preachers preach for decision. It's not automatic or implicit just because you prepare and deliver a sermon. Second, there's a relationship between a decisional emphasis in the preaching event and the decisions made by individuals who listen to preaching. In His sovereignty God mysteriously has ordained that what we do and don't do when we preach in some way affects whether or not people decide for the truth. I don't understand it and I can't explain it, but I believe it to be true. He has assigned us certain responsibilities as preachers that when carried out faithfully seem to foster spiritual decision-making. Third, the supernatural power of the Gospel and the work of the Holy Spirit somehow work in partnership with certain rhetorical principles of persuasion to create a decisional emphasis in the preaching event.

So, let's explore this issue of decisional preaching, because people don't ooze into the kingdom of God, nor do they ooze into obedience. They decide for both. And we need to give them a chance to do so.

CHAPTER I

CONFESSIONS OF A SPURGEONIST

I'm no Internet genius, but I have learned to make my way around some of the more popular sites like Google, YouTube and Twitter. Like many people today, I also spend a lot of time on Amazon. Yes, I drank the Kool-Aid of online shopping and regularly enjoy the convenience of not having to travel to the mall and fight the crowds. But on a few recent occasions I've encountered an incredibly frustrating situation while trying to make an online purchase. After arriving at the place in the process where I am ready to close the deal, the page I am looking at surprisingly doesn't have a button that says anything like "Purchase Now," "Buy now with 1-Click" or even "Add to Cart." I can't tell you how frustrating it is on those occasions to find the right merchandise, read the product information, compare the price with other vendors, sift through the reviews, decide to make the purchase, and even get excited about owning the new item, but then not be given a way to actually buy it!

I've learned that sometimes the reason for this shopping quandary is because the item I'm after isn't currently available. It's one thing to face this dilemma when trying to buy earthly and temporal products that may or may not be available. It's an entirely different thing not to be given a chance to close the deal when being confronted with spiritual and eternal truth that's always available. That's what's so tragic about preaching that doesn't include a "Buy now" or "Add to" option for listeners. The stakes are higher, so the frustration is greater. But that's exactly what happens when preachers preach the truth of God's Word, but never call on people to decide for it. We show them the right merchandise, explain the product information to them, convince them the price is right, support its validity with the fruit of our study, persuade them to believe it's a wise decision, and even lead them to a level of enthusiasm about signing on. But then we frustrate them to no end by never calling on them to actually complete the purchase! Let me see if I can help us think through this irony.

WHERE I AM AND WHY I'M THERE

"Hi, my name is Jim, and I'm a decisional schizophrenic." I admit it. I can't reconcile every aspect of my theology with the convictions I have about the subject of this book. This is a book about decisional preaching, not about decisional regeneration or even decisional theology. I believe in decisional preaching. I don't believe in decisional regeneration the way some people do. I don't believe people just "decide" to become Christians apart from the gracious, life-giving work of God's Spirit. I don't believe they can be saved by living a good life, walking an aisle, praying a canned prayer, filling out a card, being baptized or joining a church. In fact, I don't believe people can get into heaven through any system or activity that is dependent on the exercise of their own will. I believe salvation is by grace alone; it's a sovereign work of God through His Holy Spirit. I believe it happens when God determines for it to happen.

The Bible clearly teaches that people are incapable of choosing Christ. Outside of Him we are "dead in trespasses and sins" (Eph 2:1) and we "cannot please God" (Rom. 8:8). When it comes to unregenerate people, "no one seeks God" (Rom. 3:11) and no one can "accept the things of the Spirit of God . . . and he is not able to understand them" (1 Cor 2:14). There's absolutely no way a person can come to Christ "unless the Father who sent [Jesus] draws him" (John 6:44). I'm no rocket scientist (or better yet, medical doctor), but I'm pretty much thinking these verses mean lost people can't make spiritual decisions without some help. Expecting otherwise would be like asking a corpse to run a marathon.

That's why I believe salvation is totally the work of God. The Apostle Paul writes, "By works of the law no human being will be justified" (Rom 3:20). We don't choose Jesus; He chooses us (John 15:16), gives us back the life of God we were created to have (John 14:6; Rom. 6:1-14,23), and promises to preserve us forever (John 10:28). We are born again "not of blood nor of the will of the flesh nor of the will of man, but of God" (John 1:13). Jesus says, "For as the Father raises the dead and gives them life, so also the Son gives life to whom he will" (John 5:21). God is solely and sovereignly responsible for every aspect of our salvation. He even gives us the faith to believe so no one steals His glory—"For by grace you have been saved through faith. And this is not your own doing; it is the gift of God, not a result of works, so that no one may boast" (Eph 2:8-9).

Having said all that, let me muddy the waters a bit. I also firmly believe that somehow people have to reach out to God to be saved. Jesus began His public ministry by proclaiming, "Repent, for the kingdom of heaven is at hand" (Matt 4:17; cf. Mark 1:15). The apostles who lived with Him 24/7 for three years apparently adopted that same conviction. On the day of Pentecost Peter quoted from Joel 2:32 when he announced that "everyone who calls upon the name of the Lord shall be saved" (Acts 2:21; cf. Rom 10:13). On Solomon's Porch he preached that people must "repent, therefore, and turn back, that [their] sins may be blotted out" (Acts 3:19; cf. 2:38). Paul evidently reached the same conclusion because he told the Philippian jailer, "Believe in the Lord Jesus, and you will be saved" (Acts 16:31), and he announced to the men of Athens that God Himself "commands all people everywhere to repent" (Acts 17:30).

Not only do unbelievers have to respond to the Gospel in order to be saved, but believers have to respond to Gospel truth in order to grow in Christlikeness. Neither time nor space (nor necessity!) allow me to list all the imperative commands in the New Testament letters. Don't these commands logically imply the demand for a response on the part of the readers? Don't they suggest that a decision has to be made whether to obey or not obey? Based on the believer's possession of the "divine nature," the Apostle Peter exhorts,

> For this very reason, *make every effort* to supplement your faith with virtue, and virtue with knowledge, and knowledge with self-control, and self-control with steadfastness, and steadfastness with godliness, and godliness with brotherly affection, and brotherly affection with love. For if these qualities are yours and are increasing, they keep you from being ineffective or unfruitful in the knowledge

of our Lord Jesus Christ. For whoever lacks these qualities is so nearsighted that he is blind, having forgotten that he was cleansed from his former sins. Therefore, brothers, *be all the more diligent* to confirm your calling and election, for if you practice these qualities you will never fall. For in this way there will be richly provided for you an entrance into the eternal kingdom of our Lord and Savior Jesus Christ. (2 Pet 1:5–11; emphasis mine)

Why would he say these things if it wasn't imperative for his readers to decide to obey in order to progress in their journeys to Christlikeness? While it's true that phrases like "make a decision for Christ" or "accept Jesus" can't be found on the pages of the Bible, surely the fact that we are commanded to do things like "repent," "believe," "call upon," "make every effort," "be all the more diligent," and all the other exhortations in the New Testament at the very least imply that some kind of exercise of the will is in play.

So, the question you're probably asking is—How do you reconcile this stuff? Well, I don't. Seem schizophrenic? Maybe so, but I'm in good company. When Spurgeon was asked how he reconciled divine sovereignty and human responsibility, he replied, "I never have to reconcile friends. Divine sovereignty and human responsibility have never had a falling out with each other. I do not need to reconcile what God has joined together."[8] Spurgeon was honest in his acknowledgment that "where these two truths meet I do not know, nor do I want to know. They do not puzzle me, since I have given up my mind to believing them both."[9] He refused to go where Scripture does not go, but he firmly believed what Scripture says with where Scripture goes.

Spurgeon subsequently applied his conviction about this irreconcilable tension to his preaching for decisions. Regarding what some perceived to be a contradiction between preaching election and extending a call for people to respond to the Gospel, Spurgeon answered similarly: "There is no need to reconcile them, for they have never yet quarreled with one another."[10] I love what Steve Lawson said about this tension in which Spurgeon lived and preached:

> Being committed to the full counsel of God, Spurgeon embraced both truths with equal allegiance. He clung tenaciously to God's sovereignty in the salvation of His elect, but he was equally convinced of the mandate to extend the offer of the Gospel to every person. Emphasizing one of these truths to the exclusion of the other, he believed, would result in an unbalanced ministry. . . . Spurgeon simply embraced both divine sovereignty and human responsibility as clearly taught in the pages of Scripture.[11]

I think learning to live comfortably within this tension is the secret to believing wholly in the sovereignty of God in salvation and calling passionately for listeners to decide for God's truth. So if you ask me if I'm a Calvinist or an Arminian, my response is "I'm a Spurgeonist." I don't have to reconcile divine sovereignty and human responsibility, so neither do I have to reconcile divine sovereignty and decisional preaching. They're friends.

This tension allows me to be completely comfortable with the conviction that the Bible speaks with abundant clarity about the process for life transformation. God's Word does the supernatural work. Jesus prays for His followers, asking God to "sanctify them in the truth; your word is truth" (John 17:17). Paul says that "faith comes by hearing, and hearing through the word of Christ" (Rom 10:17). So we proclaim God's powerful and sufficient Word, and we confidently compel people to say "yes" to it. As they hear it and decide rightly for it, then they experience life change.

WHERE WE ARE AND WHERE WE SHOULD BE

In today's church we seem to be living through a famine of calling people to decide for the truth of God's Word. Fewer and fewer pastors are demanding that listeners render a verdict on what they've preached, whether it be within the sermon or at the end of it. There's a lot of information being communicated, but less and less appeal for listeners to say "yes" or "no" on their acceptance and application of the message. Today we have more pastors who are interpreting the text with integrity, exposing its intended meaning, and making relevant application. But at the same time, the frequency of sermons that demand a response is diminishing. The explanation and application of biblical truths—accompanied by the call for decision—often is jettisoned for the sake of conversational presentations that have more of a fireside chat feel than they do of a bold, urgent, and passionate appeal.

What has caused this drought? While only heaven knows the depth of spiritual realities that have contributed to a de-emphasis on calling for a response in the preaching event, I've noticed three particular culprits from where I sit. And all three of them have multiple tributaries, some of which I can't take the time and space to track down in detail. But these trends appear to play some role in leading many preachers to shy away from calling on listeners to decide for the truth being preached.

The first is what I would describe as a *reaction to revivalism*. Many younger preachers today have an aversion to what they perceive to be a "packaging" of evangelicalism, particularly in the revivalism of the nineteenth and twentieth centuries. In one sense, God's work through Whitefield and Wesley during the First Great Awakening gave birth to evangelicalism. People saw these "revivals" and were inspired to be more intentional about calling for conversions. Essentially, they concluded, "We can tap into this!" But regarding the Second Great Awakening, a lot of millennial preachers look with skepticism on the theology and ministry of Finney, as well as his perceived subsequent influence on the work of Moody, Sunday, and even Graham. Their assessment is that many evangelicals were no longer satisfied just saying, "We can tap into this!" Instead, they began saying, "We can create this!" Consequently, many younger preachers keep revivalism at arm's length . . . at the very least.

Let me highlight just a couple of ways this reaction to revivalism has subtly affected contemporary preaching as it relates to calling for listeners to respond. Some preachers live with a fear of false decisions. Let's be honest—as long as the church tarries on earth it will be plagued by unregenerate members, emotionalism, and manipulative appeals for people to make decisions. Jesus told us it would be this way (cf. Matt 7:15-23; 13:1-30). And there's no doubt that false converts hurt the church's witness and undermine the glory of Christ. But when the pastor is so fearful of people making false decisions, he has a tendency to pull back the throttle on asking people to make decisions at all.[12] And doing so is a breach of his responsibility to make disciples.

Similarly, the reaction to revivalism has manifested itself in the abuse of the altar call. More specifically, I'm talking about the *over-reaction* to the abuse of the altar call. All of us have seen preachers commit heinous crimes when it comes to inviting people to give immediate, public expression to spiritual responses. Preachers have used peer pressure, crowd control methods, bait-and-switch appeals, emotion-driven pleas, high-pressure sales techniques, soft Gospel presentations, soothing ambiance, and more to manipulate people to respond to altar-call invitations. Without question, antics like these are an affront to the Gospel of Christ. But instead of just correcting the abuses, or even jettisoning the altar call for some other method of expressing response, many preachers throw the baby out with the bath water. They allow the abuses to make them reluctant to compel people to respond with any kind of decision at all. This, too, is an affront to the Gospel.

A second major contributor to preaching that doesn't call for a decision is a *misapplication of Reformed theology*. Let me be clear at this point. I celebrate the Protestant Reformation and consider myself one who embraces *most* of the theological tenants that define it. But it appears that today many preachers who embrace Reformed theology take some of its principles to unnecessary ends, ones with which the early reformers likely would have been uncomfortable. These modern preachers mistakenly follow a later version of the Protestant Reformation that was set by the reformers' successors, not the early founding figures of Protestantism. I'm talking specifically about the failure to call on people to decide for the truth of God's Word.

This historic shift took place when a Scholastic way of considering biblical doctrines was infused into the later reformers' reading and appropriation of Scripture. In their scrutiny of biblical teaching, these later figures often asked questions that the early reformers never asked and posited questions that the Bible doesn't answer. This intricate inspection gave birth to an understanding of salvation that negated the need for persuasion in preaching. Most of the early reformers, however, were compelled to let Scripture speak for itself and on its own terms. This included the onus of responsibility being placed on preachers to passionately appeal for their audiences to respond to the Gospel truth throughout their sermons. Here the pulpit became a powerful tool leveraged to help move the previously passive population toward a decision and ultimately to action. Strong convictions about God's sovereignty, divine election, and predestination didn't prevent these brothers from following the biblical mandate to appeal aggressively for listeners to render a verdict regarding the demands the preached Word made on their lives.

A third influence on the demise of decisional preaching in our day is merely a *forgetfulness of the nature of preaching*. The more education and resources we have available to us, the easier it becomes to forget the irony of preaching. For all practical purposes the preaching event is a train wreck waiting to happen! God has entrusted His inerrant and infallible Word to errant and fallible preachers. How can that turn out well? While it's hard for us to fathom, God has sovereignly ordained it to be so. Nowhere is this irony more evident than in the partnership between God's supernatural message and man's natural means of communicating that message. God has chosen for His sacred Word to be orally transmitted through the laws that govern mankind's natural speech. And that means that people's decision about the message is in some mysterious way connected to the human instrument who delivers the message during the preaching event.

This relationship has been true of Christian preaching since its birth, even in its earliest influences. Hebrew prophecy gave preaching its roots in the divine and was characterized by the demand for definite choice in response to God's message. As classical rhetoric was formalized, it heightened the motif of persuasion that was already implicit.[13] Along with Cicero and Quintilian, Aristotle systematically developed rhetorical theory. He defined rhetoric "as the faculty of discovering all the possible means of persuasion in any subject."[14] But these guys didn't invent something new. Instead, they merely systematized what they observed in effective communicators. As the natural relationship between rhetoric and preaching matured, a common denominator was solidified—the persuasion of listeners to make a decision regarding the message. So, the responsibility for preachers to carry out that task has characterized faithful preaching throughout history. And it remains our mandate today.

WHAT THE BIBLE SAYS AND DOESN'T SAY

But is this mandate a *biblical* mandate? Does Scripture actually compel preachers to persuade listeners to the truth and demand they render a verdict on it? I think it does, both explicitly and implicitly. When I read the Bible, it seems clear that both Old and New Testament preachers clearly persuaded people with integrity to respond to their preaching. I'll not take the time here to examine the whole scope of Scripture, but I'll call attention to preaching on this side of the cross where we live and minister. Even a cursory consideration of the two most prominent preachers in the New Testament proves the point. First of all, Jesus invited people to respond to His message with great emotion (emphasis mine):

> *Come to me*, all who labor and are heavy laden, and I will give you rest. *Take my yoke* upon you, and *learn from me*, for I am gentle and lowly in heart, and you will find rest for

> your souls. For my yoke is easy, and my burden is light." (Matt 11:28–30)
>
> On the last day of the feast, the great day, Jesus stood up and cried out, "If anyone thirsts, *let him come to me and drink*." (John 7:37)
>
> And the master said to the servant, "Go out to the highways and hedges and *compel people to come in*, that my house may be filled." (Lk. 14:23)
>
> The Spirit and the Bride say, "*Come*." And let the one who hears say, "*Come*." And let the one who is thirsty *come*; let the one who desires *take* the water of life without price. (Rev. 22:17)

Second, the apostle Paul passionately persuaded people to decide for the truth (emphasis mine):

> And Paul went in, as was his custom, and on three Sabbath days he *reasoned with them from the Scriptures*. (Acts 17:2)
>
> So he *reasoned* in the synagogue with the Jews and the devout persons, and in the marketplace every day with those who happened to be there. (Acts 17:17)
>
> And he *reasoned* in the synagogue every Sabbath, and tried to *persuade* Jews and Greeks. (Acts 18:4)

And they came to Ephesus, and he left them there, but he himself went into the synagogue and *reasoned* with the Jews. (Acts 18:19)

And he entered the synagogue and for three months spoke boldly, *reasoning and persuading them about the kingdom of God*. But when some became stubborn and continued in unbelief, speaking evil of the Way before the congregation, he withdrew from them and took the disciples with him, *reasoning* daily in the hall of Tyrannus. (Acts 19:8–9)

And as *he reasoned about righteousness and self-control and the coming judgment*, Felix was alarmed and said, "Go away for the present. When I get an opportunity I will summon you." (Acts 24:25)

And Agrippa said to Paul, "In a short time *would you persuade me to be a Christian?*" And Paul said, "Whether short or long, *I would to God that not only you but also all who hear me this day might become such as I am*—except for these chains." (Acts 26:28–29)

When they had appointed a day for him, they came to him at his lodging in greater numbers. From morning till evening *he expounded to them, testifying to the kingdom of God and trying to convince them about Jesus* both from the Law of Moses and from the Prophets. (Acts 28:23)

> Therefore, knowing the fear of the Lord, *we persuade others*. But what we are is known to God, and I hope it is known also to your conscience. (2 Cor 5:11)

> Therefore, we are ambassadors for Christ, *God making his appeal through us. We implore you on behalf of Christ, be reconciled to God.* (2 Cor 5:20)

It's hard to read Jesus and Paul and not conclude that they constrained their listeners to make a decision about the truth's they preached. And so should we.

One of the clearest and most compelling exhortations we have in the New Testament to preach for a decision is Paul's directions to the young pastor, Timothy. He instructed him, "Until I come, devote yourself to the public reading of Scripture, to exhortation, to teaching" (1 Tim 4:13). The word *exhortation* (*paraklēsis*) is translated as "preaching" by many scholars and indicates moral instruction that appeals to the will.[15] John MacArthur says it challenges people to apply the truths they've been taught and warns them to obey it. It "always involves a binding of the conscience."[16] Ralph Earle asserts that exhortation "is an important part of every pastor's duties. He must not only read the Word of God to his people but also exhort them to obey it."[17]

This same word is translated as *encouragement* in Acts 13:15, where it's used also in correlation with the reading of Scripture: "After the reading from the Law and the Prophets, the rulers of the synagogue sent a message to them, saying, 'Brothers, if you have any word of encouragement for the people, say it.'" The word is used elsewhere in association with the Old Testament (Rom 15:4; Heb 12:5), the letter to the Jerusalem Council (Acts 15:31), and as a description of the letter to the Hebrews (Heb 13:22). The three senses recognized as inherent in the word's meaning are "to summon or ask, to exhort, and to comfort." At its heart in all of these uses is the idea of summoning hearers to respond to the Scripture that has been read.[18] That's what true preaching is about.

Before I leave this subject, let me circle back around and tie this biblical mandate to the misapplication of Reformed theology that I mentioned earlier. It's no secret that Spurgeon was Reformed in his theology. But at the very same time, he was perfectly comfortable living in the tension between strong Reformed convictions and passionate biblical persuasion. He says, "Some of my brethren are greatly scandalized by the general invitations which I am in the habit of giving to sinners, as sinners. Some of them go the length of asserting that there are no universal invitations in the Word of God."[19] And again,

> I know the Lord has blessed my appeals to all sorts of sinners and none shall stop me in giving free invitations as long as I find them in this Book. And I do cry with Peter this morning to this vast assembly, "Repent and be baptized, every one of you, in the name of the Lord Jesus. For the promise is unto you and to your children, even to as many as the Lord our God shall call."[20]

To the dismay of some of his Calvinist colleagues, Spurgeon was a fan of inviting people to respond to the Gospel. He states, "I further believe, although certain persons deny it, that the influence of fear is to be exercised over the minds of men, and that it ought to operate upon the mind of the preacher himself."[21] While this is not a suggestion that Spurgeon supported or practiced public altar calls, he apparently believed that preachers should apply pressure and emotion to compel people to respond to the Gospel.

There are some things about which God didn't give us all the information we'd like to have. The Bible doesn't reconcile for us all the mysteries of God's sovereignty and man's will. And when we force ourselves to reconcile the unsolvable mysteries in Scripture, we back ourselves into a corner and end up disobeying things that are clear in God's Word. And God's Word is clear that the Gospel demands a response. Consequently, preachers have a responsibility to give their listeners an opportunity to render one.

WHAT THIS BOOK ISN'T AND IS

This is a book about decisional preaching. But please understand that I'm not talking about preachers just calling on unbelievers to decide for Christ. Certainly, the call for decision often has been limited to the persuasion of lost people to do just that. This aspect of a decisional emphasis has helped to make preaching an important evangelistic tool in my own denomination. That's why for many preachers in our tradition, it naturally has followed that the sermon include a call for an immediate and public response to the message proclaimed. One of the distinctive qualities of evangelistic preaching has been the call for a decision for Christ based upon the kerygmatic content of the message.

This book, however, isn't about convincing preachers to give an altar-call invitation. I certainly believe that can be done with integrity, which I'll address later. When I use the term *decisional preaching*, however, I'm talking about Spirit-empowered preaching that's intentional and aggressive in calling every listener to respond to Gospel truth. Decisional preaching is aimed at seeing both believers and unbelievers respond positively to the preached Word by offering a faith response to whatever truth is being presented.

No doubt, the emergence of contemporary communication theory in the second half of the twentieth century had some negative influences on preaching. One of its benefits, however, was that it helped to revive a holistic view of preaching as being decisional in nature. Many homileticians began to view the call for decision as broader than the invitation to salvation. Daniel J. Baumann, for example, says,

> preaching worthy of the name calls persons to a decision, to a confrontation which hopefully issues in modification of behavior. This behavior change may take any number of directions including salvation, vocation, adoration, praise, confession, baptism, church membership, service within the life of the community, or wholeness regarding psychological and emotional health. Explicit preaching is directed toward life-style changes. Preaching fails when it allows the listener to be neutral or indifferent.[22]

True preaching calls people to a make a decision. And prayerfully that decision is to obey the truth of God's Word, which subsequently will result in life transformation.

So this is a book about seeing the whole sermon as an invitation for people—both believers and non-believers—to say "yes" to whatever Gospel truth is being preached. MacArthur identifies this aim as the goal of preaching:

> I believe the goal of preaching is to compel people to make a decision. I want people who listen to me to understand exactly what God's Word demands of them when I am

through. Then they must say either, "Yes, I will do what God says," or "No, I won't do what God says."[23]

And I love how Allen puts it:

> A better way—and, I believe, a more biblical way—is for the sermon to be an invitation. Seeking to persuade is integral to biblical preaching. . . . If you haven't invited, you haven't preached. If you haven't persuaded, you haven't preached. If you haven't begged, you haven't preached. You may have lectured, led an inductive Bible study, or presented an insightful exposition, but to be a preacher is to be a pleader, a persuader, a beggar.[24]

In order for people to decide for the glorious Gospel, preachers must clearly and convincingly give them an opportunity.

SUMMARY

So that's my argument for decisional preaching. It's not perfect, and it's not exhaustive. But I think it at least establishes merit for our consideration of the subject. But it's one thing to know what decisional preaching is and why we should do it. It's another thing to know how to do it. So let's turn our attention to that undertaking. In the following chapters I've set out to accomplish three tasks. First, I want us to think about some elements we need to include in our preparation to do decisional preaching (chapter 2). Next, I want to identify some decisional qualities of sermon development and delivery (chapters 3–5). Then I'll finish by addressing the much-debated topic of calling for people to give physical expressions of response to the preached Word (chapter 6). For each of these categories I'll try to draw some implications that will challenge us preachers to embrace and practice decisional preaching. I pray this journey helps us all be preachers who call for people to decide rightly for the truth of the Gospel.

CHAPTER II

PREPARING TO CALL FOR DECISIONS

This chapter may not be about what you think. Most of the time when we talk about "preparation" for preaching, we're referring to the process of sermon making—studying the text, developing an outline, finding illustrations, writing a manuscript, etc. All those things and more actually are part of the preparation process, and I'm going to address some of them in the coming chapters. However, when we think about decisional preaching, some aspects of the preparation process that are particularly important often are overlooked.

To introduce you to these important aspects of preaching preparation, let me call your attention to a familiar Bible passage. When the aged apostle Paul was writing to encourage young Pastor Timothy not to quit, one of the things he talked to him about was the role Scripture played in his life and work. He says,

> But as for you, continue in what you have learned and have firmly believed, knowing from whom you learned it and

> how from childhood you have been acquainted with the sacred writings, which are able to make you wise for salvation through faith in Christ Jesus. All Scripture is breathed out by God and profitable for teaching, for reproof, for correction, and for training in righteousness, that the man of God may be complete, equipped for every good work. I charge you in the presence of God and of Christ Jesus, who is to judge the living and the dead, and by his appearing and his kingdom: preach the word; be ready in season and out of season; reprove, rebuke, and exhort, with complete patience and teaching. (2 Tim 3:14–4:2)

From Paul's exhortation we can draw three general conclusions. First, inspired Scripture possesses the capacity to transform lives ("able . . . profitable . . . complete . . . equipped"). Second, people should devote themselves to it ("continue in"). Third, preaching should call people to devote themselves to it ("preach the word . . . reprove, rebuke, and exhort").

One of the most overlooked—yet obvious—aspects of the 2 Timothy passage is that its first application is to pastors. We often jump immediately in our preaching to how Scripture is profitable for teaching, reproving, correcting, and training *our people* in righteousness. And while that's true, Paul actually was calling Timothy's attention to Scripture's benefit for him as a "man of God" (2 Tim 3:17), which was an Old Testament designation of God's prophet. Because Scripture is "able to make you wise for salvation" (2 Tim 3:15) and "competent, equipped for every good work" (2 Tim 3:17), as well as accomplish all of the benefits mentioned above, pastors are to "continue in" it (2 Tim 3:14).

If the Holy Spirit inspired a book that's capable of fostering this kind of life transformation, then that book and the One who wrote it should be the primary influences on the preacher, the sermon, and the listeners. As a preacher of God's Word, and one who desires people to decide rightly about His truth, it's easy for me to overlook the place the Holy Spirit and the inspired Scripture have in my own life. I can't expect my preaching to be effectual in fostering life change if I'm not deciding rightly about these two realities and allowing them to play their proper role in my own life as well as in the sermons I preach. Based on these truths, let me point out two factors that need to be present as we prepare to preach decisionally.

IMMERSION IN THE SCRIPTURE

If people who listen to us preach are going to decide rightly for God's truth, it will only be because His Spirit enables them to do so. That being the case, preachers need to make sure that God's Spirit is permeating their lives from A to Z in the preaching event. And since the Holy Spirit inspired Scripture, then Scripture must drive every aspect of our lives, beginning with our personal walks and extending all the way to our public proclamation. Our lives and ministries must be immersed in Scripture.

Ezra, the Old Testament scribe, provides a simple yet profound model for a shepherd who immerses his life and ministry in the very Scriptures he desires to teach to his people. The Bible tells us that "Ezra had set his heart to study the Law of the Lord, and to do it and to teach his statutes and rules in Israel" (Ezra 7:10). What he taught, he first lived. What he lived was determined by the Scriptures he studied. He put study, conduct, and teaching in the right order so each component of his life was able to function properly at its best. Kidner observes that Ezra's "study was saved from unreality, conduct from uncertainty, and teaching from insincerity and shallowness."[25]

Ezra devoted all of himself and all his life to the wonderful ministry of God's Word. He immersed himself in it. The regular routine of study, obedience and teaching was the secret of his impact on the people. Because he loved God's Word, he loved God's people and desired for them to know and embrace Him wholeheartedly. So let's look at how we can apply Ezra's example in our lives so people are best positioned to decide rightly for God's Word when we preach it.

Study the Bible

I've been preaching for over thirty-five years now. And because I started pastoring early in my journey, there haven't been many seasons in those years when I didn't have a sermon to prepare for Sunday. I've been blessed to be able to preach just about every week, which has driven me into the study of God's Word every week. And that's a good thing. Or is it? Several years ago I started asking myself the question, "Would I be studying the Bible this much every week if I didn't have a sermon to prepare?" While it's certainly a good thing anytime we study the Bible, it's easy for me to fall into the rut of just studying the Bible because I have to preach.

As I began to assess my motivation for studying God's Word, I resolved to shift my focus. While I've been called to preach, I don't want that to be the primary incentive for driving me into the Scriptures. I want to study the Bible because I want to know Christ more and get more of His effectual presence working in my life. I don't want to study the Bible because I have to preach; I want to preach because I study the Bible! I want to be compelled to preach because I'm consumed and compelled by the Scriptures. I want what I hear from God in the quiet place to burn so hot in my heart that I have to preach it. I want to preach because I'm in love with Christ and want everyone else to be in love with Him, too.

That's what Ezra did. He devoted himself to "study" (Ezra 7:.10) —to make a careful search—of God's written revelation. He understood that God had created everything through His Word, that He directs history by it, and that He reveals Himself through it.[26] So Ezra dedicated his life to careful study of the Scriptures so He could know God and help others to do the same. Ezra's ministry was built on the foundation of His personal encounter with God. It was there that he developed a healthy and humble dependence on Him. And that's what we must do. Preaching for right decisions about Christ begins on our knees before an open Bible.

The power and presence of God in the pastor's ministry must be pursued first in the pastor's walk with God. Though the effects of the Spirit's work often aren't noticed until the preacher delivers his sermon, the man of God must build his entire preaching ministry on the Spirit's presence in his life. And that presence begins long before the sermon-building process begins. Jason Meyer says, "The preacher's study must be anointed, not just the pulpit."[27] The preacher must pursue the Spirit's help in bringing people to spiritual decisions well in advance of the actual preaching event. He must pursue it even in his personal study of God's Word.

Before we can expect people to decide rightly for God's truth, we have to be caught up in it ourselves. When that happens, preparing sermons will take its rightful place as the natural outgrowth of our personal walks with God. We won't be getting the cart before the horse, thinking too much about preparing and presenting a sermon and too little about hearing God's voice as He speaks to us. Our sermons ought to be birthed in our personal encounters with God![28] If you're going to expect the Scriptures to affect the lives of your people so they can decide rightly for truth, then you need to know the Author of those Scriptures intimately. When you get closely acquainted with Jesus and fall in love with Him, that relationship will show up in your preaching. Don't lose God in your study, preacher! Develop and nurture a vibrant practice of personal worship.

Your personal study in the Bible should ultimately inform the way you study to preach. In both pursuits your ultimate goal is to hear God's voice. So as you seek to meet God in His Word, make sure you're listening rightly. You can't presume the Spirit will be operative in your preaching if you handle His book flippantly or nonchalantly.

If Scripture is truly breathed out by God through His Holy Spirit, then we are compelled to study the Bible in such a way that rightly represents what He intended to say. If you want God's Spirit to empower you as you preach and affect your listeners positively, then it just makes sense that you should give yourself to studying His Word with integrity. If the Holy Spirit inspired the Bible, then it makes no sense that we would expect Him to attend to our preaching if we treat His words lightly or use them for some other purpose than what He intended.[29]

A commitment to study the Bible with integrity naturally involves a process that will serve as the foundation for biblical preaching. That process begins with applying right principles of interpretation in careful Bible study where we seek to "draw out" God's intended meaning in a given passage. While interpretation involves the principles and methods for understanding Scripture, our actual study of a passage is the process of applying those principles and methods to the text. So Bible study essentially is the application of your interpretative lens in order to help you discover the right meaning of a passage.[30] Your responsibility is to discover what God says in every text of Scripture and then draw it out so you can proclaim it to others. Then and only then will they be able to know what God demands of them and decide for it accordingly.

Obey the Bible

Ezra didn't just set his heart to study the Scriptures, he devoted himself to "do it" (Ezra 7:.10). Neither our study of the Bible nor our preaching of it will have any value if we don't obey what God says and allow it to shape our lives. When we study the Bible, we hear God's voice. When we obey the Bible, we flesh out God's voice in daily living. If we want our listeners to be doers of God's Word—to say "yes" to its demands on their lives—then we need to demonstrate as much by doing the same. We must be and do what we want our listeners to be and do.

Obeying God's Word as lifestyle naturally issues forth into a life of practical holiness, which is imperative for preaching God's Word in the power of His Spirit. God's attendance to your preaching doesn't start when you get up to preach. It starts in your personal communion with Him, but then it extends into your daily walk and interaction with people. That's why the Bible says to "purify yourselves, you who bear the vessels of the Lord" (Isa. 52:11). Just like it makes no sense that we would expect the Holy Spirit to empower our preaching if we neglect the Book He inspired, it's inconceivable for us to presume on His strong help if we make a mockery of the vessels He inhabits. God desires to use clean lives as conduits of His enabling power.

Two of the manifestations of holiness are the related qualities of character and integrity. Character refers to moral excellence and firmness. Integrity is the firm adherence to a code of moral values. Together, they're describing the degree to which we adhere to God's standard of moral excellence. Paul charged Timothy to "keep a close watch on yourself and on the teaching" (1 Tim 4:16). In both 1 Timothy 3:1-7 and Titus 1:5-9 he provides somewhat of a heart checkup for pastors, and in 1 Thessalonians 2:1-12 he speaks intimately and personally about some benchmarks of pastoral leadership characterized by character and integrity. As preachers, we have to decide whether or not we will match our manner with our message, our life with our lips, and what we are with what we say.

If we try to preach decisionally while living in disobedience, God's Word will not flow through us with power, and neither will it be received with any effectual force. The author of Proverbs observes that "a muddied spring or a polluted fountain is a righteous man who gives way before the wicked" (Prov 25:26). When a well is polluted, you can't clean it out or purify it. You just have to cap it. When a preacher's life is contaminated with the pollution of the world, people stop drinking from his well. The author of Hebrews instructs us to "strive for peace with everyone, and for the holiness without which no one will see the Lord" (Heb. 12:14). Do a spiritual reality check every day so you can be a clean mouthpiece through whom the Lord can speak.

Preach the Bible

Because Ezra studied God's Word and then obeyed it, then and only then was he in a position to teach "his statues and rules in Israel" (Ezra 7:.10). And so he devoted himself to teaching all the requirements of God's law to the people. The more time passes and the farther we get from when and where God's revelation was given, the more the community of faith will need men to perform this service. Proclaiming God's Word is much more than just giving a bunch of information. It involves maturing people into Christ's image, training them in righteousness, and spurring them on to love and obedience. It's the only way believers are able to develop a biblical lens through which to interpret the world and to know how to live their daily lives.

If studying the Bible enables preachers to hear God's voice and obeying the Bible enables preachers to flesh out God's voice, then preaching the Bible has to be done in a way that listeners are able to hear and do the same. That means that preaching today must be expository in nature. Why? Because the word *exposition* comes from the root verb "to expose." It means to lay open or uncover. When a preacher is doing exposition, he is laying open and uncovering the voice of God in a given biblical text so people can hear it and obey it. The only way people can decide for God's truth rightly is if they first hear it accurately.

To lean into this a bit more, I think expository preaching is *the process of laying open the biblical text in such a way that the Holy Spirit's intended meaning and accompanying power are brought to bear on the lives of contemporary listeners.* When contemporary listeners hear the voice of God rightly, it comes to bear on their lives and they have to decide for it. The only way that's going to happen is if a preacher peels back the layers of time, language, culture, and other factors so they can see God's intended meaning in whatever passage is under consideration. As the preacher faithfully expounds a Bible text in his preaching, the Holy Spirit does two things: 1) He empowers the preacher to explain and apply the text accurately, and 2) He enables listeners to respond to it rightly.

There's no greater need in the church of Jesus Christ today than for more men to step up and answer this high calling to expose the voice of God to people through the preaching of His Word. Mankind has no greater need than to hear God's voice clearly and respond to it positively. Preaching is God's primary plan for the propagation of the Gospel and the re-creation of people into Christ's image. When the

Bible is preached rightly, listeners have the opportunity to assess it and decide for it with the help of God's Spirit.

ATTENDANCE OF THE SPIRIT

To be completely honest, I'm a fish out of water when it comes to being a seminary professor. I don't consider myself an academician. In fact, I really don't even like to read. It's hard work for me. When I first started seminary as a student, I actually swore that I would never do doctoral work and that I would never teach. Through some disillusioning events in my first pastorate, however, God brought me to an awareness of something that's haunted me my entire ministry. I realized that I could actually carry out my entire ministry as a pastor in a way that people observing me would consider me to be effective and successful, only to get to the end and find out I had done every bit of it completely devoid of any other-worldly power. That scared me to death! And it still does.

That's what led me to become a seminary professor. God used that crisis to develop a burden in my heart to want to get in a context where I could have that conversation with young preachers. So I went back to school to get the credentials I needed to be on the faculty of a Bible college or seminary. More than doing research, writing books, or even teaching young guys how to preach, I've wanted to talk to them about the deception of being influential leaders that crowds want to follow, gifted administrators that develop cutting-edge programs, dynamic speakers that masses flock to hear, and charismatic personalities to which multitudes are drawn, all without any dependence on the supernatural power of the Holy Spirit.

If anything supernatural is to happen in our preaching, it's only because God's Spirit shows up and attends to it. If our listeners are going to decide rightly for the Gospel truth that we preach, it will only be because the Spirit helps them to do so. Why? Because from beginning to end, preaching is His work. John Knox says, "True preaching from start to finish is the work of the Spirit."[31] Not only did He inspire the Word we preach, but He also does the work of helping us and our listeners as we actually engage in the preaching event. Let me offer four ways preachers should intentionally and aggressively pray for the Holy Spirit to foster right decisions when we preach.

Pray for Him to Illuminate Minds

If sinful people are going to understand God's Word rightly so they can decide for it rightly, they're going to have to have some help. And that help comes from the Holy Spirit, who illuminates people's minds to mentally and spiritually understand the meaning and significance of biblical truth. He gives them insight into the meaning of the text being preached. He's not giving them new information, because the information has been right there in the Bible all the time. Instead, He's giving them a deeper understanding of the meaning that's there. This new insight sometimes comes suddenly and dramatically and at other times more gradually and quietly. But always it enables a listener to experience the Bible in a deeper sense and with a deeper level of perception. It's kind of like seeing with the heart.[32]

Everybody in the preaching event needs the help of illumination that only the Spirit can give. The Holy Spirit works by illuminating the minds of both preacher and listener to a right understanding of his preaching text. Mohler says, "Both the preacher and the hearers are dependent upon the work of the Holy Spirit for any adequate understanding of the text."[33] Prayerfully, the preacher receives illumination to his preaching passage as he studies and prepares. The listeners receive illumination as they listen to the sermon and process it in the days following its delivery.

The Bible gives us some examples of illumination. It's what happened to the disciples when they heard Jesus expound the Scriptures on the road to Emmaus (cf. Luke 24:13–35). After he disappeared from their midst, they concluded, "Did not our hearts burn within us while he talked to us on the road, while he opened to us the Scriptures?" (Luke 24:32). Jesus, in the power of the Holy Spirit, opened their minds to the truth of Scripture and its relevance for their lives. The Apostle Paul recognized the need people have for the Spirit to help with understanding spiritual truth. He says, "The natural person does not accept the things of the Spirit of God, for they are folly to him, and he is not able to understand them because they are spiritually discerned" (1 Cor 2:14). Spiritually dead people don't have the capacity to respond to spiritual prompting on their own.

As preachers who desire people to decide for Gospel truth, we have to understand that this indispensable work of illumination by the Holy Spirit won't happen without prayer. So pray first for illumination for yourself as you study your text. Certainly don't neglect your Bible study resources as part of your sermon preparation, but know that no commentary, lexicon, or Bible encyclopedia can give you what only the Spirit will give you in response to prayer. You're not ready to preach until you have sought the illuminating help of the Spirit for the purposes of correctly understanding and expounding your passage. And after you pray for your own illumination, pray for the Spirit to give it to the people who will listen to you preach. The Spirit's help with illumination is the only way your preaching can affect spiritual decision-making in your hearers.

Pray for Him to Convict Hearts

Not only does the Holy Spirit illuminate people's minds to truth, He also convicts them as they hear it proclaimed. Jesus said that when the Spirit came, "he [would] convict the world concerning sin and righteousness and judgment" (John 16:8). The word *convict* means to bring to light, expose, refute, or convince with a view toward correction. The verb occurs eighteen times in the New Testament, and in every instance it has to do with showing someone his or her sin, usually as a summons to repentance.[34] Brothers, that's huge when it comes to decisional preaching! Conviction involves the Spirit's work of bringing people to the realization that God is right and they are wrong, and wooing them to decide accordingly.

This means that when we preach in the power of the Holy Spirit, He convinces people that something other-worldly is taking place. Paul highlights this work of the Spirit with the hypothetical scenario of an unbeliever coming into a Christian worship service where—upon hearing God's Word—"he is convicted by all, he is called to account by all, the secrets of his heart are disclosed, and so, falling on his face, he will worship God and declare that God is really among you" 1 Cor. 14:24-25). Wow! When the Holy Spirit convicts people, He convinces them that God is talking and not a man!

So pray diligently for that to happen when you preach. Pray for God to let people hear His voice, to convict them, and to grant them repentance. Pray that this will happen to both believers and unbelievers. Pray for the Spirit to bring people to the conviction that the argument you're making is true and that they will be judged on the basis of whether they agree or disagree. And pray for them to decide to agree!

Pray for Him to Apply Truth

Another work of God's Spirit is applying the Bible's truth to both the preacher and the listener. It's good to know that we're not alone in this aspect of the preaching event, especially since we're preaching to people who are used to listening to gifted communicators on television, radio and podcast, but who often have little Bible knowledge or familiarity with Bible terminology. Application is a tall order in contemporary preaching!

The Holy Spirit, however, is here to help. He provides divine assistance in connecting the ancient text to life today. He arouses deep desires for listeners to know truth. He makes people aware of their sin, convinces them that Christ's work is sufficient, and gives them a desire for His salvation. He provides guidance regarding the infinite number of specific situations and problems people face. As we are faithful to expose God's voice in His Word, His Spirit is faithful to make specific application to the listeners at just the right time and just the right way.

While this doesn't negate the preacher's responsibility to make good and right application in his sermons, it does take the pressure off of him to be an expert in everything under the sun! Our relevance in preaching isn't defined and determined by what we or our listeners think is relevant, but by what the Spirit of God has determined to be relevant in the Word of God. Consequently, we're dependent on the Spirit's purpose in every text to determine our purpose in our sermons. Remember, Paul says the Spirit's aim through Scripture is to make people "complete, thoroughly equipped" (2 Tim 3:17), and the means by which He accomplishes this is through our "teaching . . . reproof . . . correction . . . training" (2 Tim 3:16). The only way real life transformation happens is when we depend on Him to accomplish the purpose that He's foreordained in Scripture.

Fellow preacher, pray for the Holy Spirit to make His timely application to the people who hear you preach. Pray for Him to foster Christlike character in them. Ask Him to help you interpret the Scripture, capture its practical and devotional nature, and bring its life-changing truths to bear on the daily lives and needs of your hearers. And ask Him to bring about the desired change in their lives. Be confident that your accurate exposition of biblical truth—delivered in the power of God's Spirit—will bring conviction on your listeners. Ask the Spirit to go to the next step and connect God's truth to people's lives. Pray for Him to help you give a clear, persuasive exposition of God's Word as well as to foster a positive response on the part of those who hear.

Pray for Him to Empower You

I pray God never stops haunting me with the awareness that I can fake my way through my entire ministry without any dependence on His Spirit. That frightening reality compels us to ask the question, "How can such a misleading ministry happen?" Let me point out three reasons.

First, we forget that God's economy is strength through weakness. Sometimes when I'm preaching, I catch myself thinking, "Why doesn't someone just shoot me and get this over with!" We all know what it means to preach in our own strength and without the power of the Holy Spirit. We know we are weak and finite vessels. When we're depending on human strength and skill, there's no life. Why? Because God has chosen to operate according to what appears to be a twisted economy: to release His strength through our weakness (cf. 1 Sam 16:7; Prov 31:30; Zech 4:6; Matt 20:16; Mark 8:34–35; 1 Cor 2:3–4; 2 Cor 4:7; 12:9–10). He's set it up this way for one reason, and that's so that when He releases His supernatural power to accomplish other-worldly things, He's the only one who gets the glory! That means we can actually rest—and even revel—in our human weakness because that's the key to accessing the Spirit's supernatural power, a power that we desperately need.

A second reason we have powerless ministries is we don't realize the difference between the availability of the Spirit's fullness for all believers and His filling for the preacher. All Christians are called to be full of the Spirit and to bear His fruit (e.g., Acts 6:3, 5; 11:24; Gal 5:22–25; Eph 5:18–21). The New Testament, however, speaks of a special attendance of God's Spirit specifically to the preaching event. While we often refer to this help as His *anointing* or *unction*, the New Testament calls it the Spirit's *filling*. Eight times in the Luke-Acts narratives (cf. Luke 1:15, 41, 67; Acts 2:4; 4:8, 31; 9:17; 13:9) the verbal form *filled* is best translated by the idea of "that which fills or takes possession of the mind."[35] The language of the New Testament suggests these instances are to be distinguished from similar descriptions in Luke-Acts translated "full, to make full, or to fill" (see Luke 4:1; Acts 6:3, 5; 7:55; 11:24; 13:52).[36] This filling of the Spirit for the preacher is "an event, a sovereign and spontaneous act of God related to the proclamation of truth."[37] In other words, just because you're a Christian preacher, are indwelt by the Holy Spirit, and walk in His fullness doesn't mean He'll automatically attend to your preaching. He wants to fill you with "an instantaneous, sudden, and sovereign operation of the Spirit of God coming upon a man so that his proclamation of Jesus Christ might be attended by holy power."[38]

A third reason I'll mention for preachers operating without the Spirit's power is that we stop asking for it. Jesus wasn't silent about the fact that God has ordained prayer to be the primary trigger that engages the Spirit in our lives effectually. When His apostles asked Him to teach them to pray (cf. Luke 11:1), Jesus ultimately responded by stating, "How much more will the heavenly Father give the Holy Spirit to those who ask him!" (Luke 11:13). When He was comforting them in view of His impending departure, He told them they would do greater redemptive works than He did during His time on earth because He was going to the Father to pour out His Spirit on them (cf. John 14:12). Then He immediately said, "Whatever you ask in my name, this I will do, that the Father may be glorified in the Son. If you ask me anything in my name, I will do it" (John 12:13-14). The indwelling of God's Spirit in every believer isn't synonymous with His effects and influences. We have to ask for it!

If you put these three oversights together, you'll arrive at a compelling argument for us to acknowledge and express our utter dependence and desperation for God's Spirit to attend to our preaching. So, dear brother, don't presume upon His work in your preaching by assuming it's automatic because you walk in His fullness. Pray diligently for Him to leverage your weakness and come upon you in His great power. Spend time seeking His face and asking Him to give you the advantage that separates preachers from all other public communicators. Plead with Him to make your words pointed, sharp, and piercing. Ask Him to give you freedom and simplicity of speech. Cry out to Him to grant you His mysterious attendance as you proclaim His Word rightly. Appeal to Him to put God in your sermon and on you, and to keep you aware of a power not your own. Pray for Him to "possess" you that you may be caught up in the message by His power.

In my own ministry I have found it helpful to use biblical truths as I pray for the Spirit to empower me in my preaching. For example, I frequently will pray that it will be for me the way it was for the apostle

Paul at Corinth: "I was with you in weakness and in fear and much trembling, and my speech and my message were not in plausible words of wisdom, but in demonstration of the Spirit and of power" (1 Cor 2:3-4). I plead with God's Spirit to use my weakness, fear, and trembling. I ask Him to prevent my sermon from being palatable words that result from my own wisdom. I ask Him to take all of my inadequacies and transform them into a clear demonstration of His power. I sometimes pray what Paul requested the Ephesians to pray, "that words may be given to me in opening my mouth boldly to proclaim the mystery of the Gospel . . . that I may declare it boldly, as I ought to speak" (Eph 6:19-20). I ask the Spirit to give me boldness that is beyond my ability.

As you pray for the Spirit's attendance to your preaching, don't just ask Him to help you. Ask Him to help your people as well. His power does something to both preacher and people. So pray that those who listen to you preach will be gripped, moved, and convicted. Pray that the Spirit will take over as you preach so that something miraculous happens in every listener's life. Pray every person in the room will become convinced that what they're hearing when you preach are not the words of a man but the very voice of God (cf. 1 Cor 2:5). Whenever I'm preparing to preach, I always pray that God will cause my listeners to experience what those disciples on the road to Emmaus experienced: "They said to each other, 'Did not our hearts burn within us while he talked to us on the road, while he opened to us the Scriptures?'" (Luke 24:32). I pray that God's Spirit will cause their hearts to burn within them to the point they become convinced that He's talking and decide to align their lives with what He's saying.

E. M. Bounds writes, "This anointing comes to the preacher not in the study but in the closet."[39] Fellow preacher, in all your learning, learn how to get hold of God's Spirit in prayer in the secret place as part of your preparation to preach. Earnestly seek His power and the passion that comes from His inspiration. Diligently ask Him to come upon you and your message. Allow Him to manifest His power in and through you. Don't be satisfied with anything less in your preaching. While you won't always experience His power to the same degree every time you preach, you can surrender your life to the Spirit in such a way that it's evident His favor is on you.

One final thing: Don't think the Spirit's power can be accessed with short, flippant prayers. And, don't think you can grab hold of Him by just praying along the way in your busy life. Make time to be long with God in pursuit of other-worldly power. Jesus says, "And I tell you, ask, and it will be given to you; seek, and you will find; knock, and it will be opened to you. For everyone who asks receives, and the one who seeks finds, and to the one who knocks it will be opened" (Luke 11:9–10). The verb tenses are present, indicating continual and repeated action: "Ask, and keep on asking; seek, and keep on seeking; knock, and keep on knocking." Otherwise, you can't expect power that reaps eternal fruit. As Bounds says,

> Prayer, much prayer, is the price of preaching unction. Prayer, much prayer, is the sole condition of keeping this anointing. Without unceasing prayer, the anointing never comes to the preacher. Without perseverance in prayer, the anointing, like overkept manna, breeds worms.[40]

Brothers, let's tarry long in asking God's Spirit to attend our preaching so that our listeners will decide rightly for Him.

SUMMARY

People can spot a fake a mile away. They know when the guy who's preaching to them is a fraud. They may not articulate it that way or even process it in those terms, but they know when something supernatural is happening, and they know when it's not. God uses us in spite of ourselves, but we can never presume upon that grace. As preachers, we have a responsibility to assume that no authentic decision-making is going to take place in our preaching if we come to the pulpit in the flesh—not having been in the counsel of God and not having pursued the help of His Spirit. Brothers, calling for decisions starts long before we ever get up to preach. Let's make sure we're prepared to do it because we've postured ourselves for God to prepare us.

CHAPTER III

DECISIONAL QUALITIES OF SERMON FOUNDATION

God's truth as recorded in Scripture and empowered by His Spirit is the only thing that has any power to change anybody's life. The truth of the Gospel is God's power for both the salvation of sinners and the sanctification of saints (cf. Rom 1:16; John 17:17). It's the primary agent the Holy Spirit uses to re-create people into the image of His Son and our Savior, Jesus Christ. When I talk about persuading people to make a decision for the truth, I do it against the backdrop of understanding that it's only God's Spirit using God's truth that can actually bring about real transformation.

With that in mind, let's consider three areas of sermon development that particularly foster genuine spiritual transformation—the foundation, the function, and the force. And certain qualities of each of these elements seem to lend themselves to calling for decisions with integrity. In this chapter we'll start with the foundation of the message. I think two areas inform a decisional foundation to every sermon. One, the sermon has to be focused on the biblical text and its Gospel message. Two, the sermon has to be formed from beginning to end in a way that reflects a call to decide for that Gospel message.

SERMON FOCUS

The focus of every sermon should be the Gospel of Jesus Christ. Of the three primary factors that influenced the development of Christian preaching—ancient oratory and rhetoric, Hebrew prophecy, and the Christian Gospel—it was the latter that served as the primary originating cause because it gave preaching its distinctive, supernatural, life-transforming content. When preachers apply principles of rhetoric to the presentation of that message, we're simply employing ways of convincing and persuading people to make a decision about it.[41] We're not asking them to decide for us, but for the Gospel message. So, the focus of our sermons must be on the actual Scripture we're preaching if we expect people to respond rightly. That means our sermons must be text-driven messages that expound the Gospel themes dictated by Scripture. So let me offer these challenges to help us focus our sermons toward decisions for the Gospel.

Let Your Text Drive Your Sermon

Sermons that foster life change are driven by the supernatural text of inspired Scripture. The word *text* implies a web. Applied to the preaching event, it suggests that the biblical text provides the basic threads with which a sermon is developed. This practice became commonplace for religious discourses after the recognition of a body of inspired Scripture.[42] Subsequently, decisional value in your preaching will be in direct relationship to your sermon's roots in the biblical text as well as how you handle the text when you study and preach it. In essence, you will influence decision-making by building your messages on the biblical text.

The biblical text is the primary change agent in the preaching event. Bryan Chapell says the text is the avenue through which the Holy Spirit impacts listeners:

> When we proclaim the Word we bring the work of the Holy Spirit to bear on others' lives. No truth grants greater encouragement in our preaching and gives us more cause to expect results from our efforts. The work of the Spirit is as inextricably linked to preaching as heat is to the light a bulb emits. When we present the light of God's Word, his Spirit performs God's purposes of warming, melting, and conforming hearts to his will.[43]

The text-driven sermon is the agent through which the Spirit of God calls people to decision. So, preaching a biblical text is "the only safe foundation for calling men to a changed life-style."[44]

Again, the role of God's Spirit in this endeavor can't be underestimated. I love the way Donald Miller highlights the decisional impact of preaching a biblical text under the leadership of the Holy Spirit. He describes preaching as "an act wherein the living truth of some portion of Holy Scripture, understood in the light of solid exegetical and historical study and made a living reality to the preacher by the Holy Spirit, comes alive to the hearer as he is confronted by God in

Christ through the Holy Spirit in judgment and redemption."[45] Such a text-based, Spirit-empowered approach is true *biblical preaching*, the only kind of legitimate preaching. Biblical preaching is the only preaching that can legitimately affect listeners. God promises to bless His Word only, not the cleverness or eloquence of the preacher. We're simply given the task of faithfully interpreting and applying the text of Scripture.

Expose the Spirit's Intended Meaning of Your Text

If decisional sermons are text-driven, then it follows that they should be treated expositorily. As I said in the previous chapter, I believe exposition is the process of laying open a text in such a way that God's intended meaning is 'exposed' to our listeners. The process demands two responsibilities on the part of the preacher. First, he must discover what God was intending to say when He inspired the text by applying right hermeneutical principles to his Bible study. Then he must plainly expose that meaning to contemporary hearers through clear explanation and relevant application.

Expository treatment of biblical texts has implicit decisional value. It's through encounters with God's voice in Scripture that our listeners hear the Word, receive it, obey it, and experience change. Harold Bryson writes:

> An expositor ought to expect life transformation as a result of preaching God's Word. Lives can be impacted and changed when God's Word is preached. Of course, transformation does not happen without human response. When the Word is preached, it needs to be heard. Just hearing the

Word stops short. It needs to be obeyed. If God's Word is heard and heeded, life transformation takes place.[46]

As we've already noted, life transformation is rooted in the power of proclaimed Scripture combined with the work of the Holy Spirit, not in the skills of the preacher. Expository preaching is the most effective way to subject people to this supernatural, life-changing combination.[47]

Haddon Robinson asserts that much modern preaching evokes little more than a wide yawn, much less a decision. Through the exposition of Scripture, God encounters individuals to draw them to salvation and Christian maturity. "Something awesome happens when God confronts an individual through preaching and seizes him by the soul."[48]

The most potent exposition happens when a preacher explains and applies a particular passage of Scripture unified by a primary theme. Broadus considers unity the primary requirement for effectualness:

> Unity in a discourse is necessary to instruction, to conviction, and to persuasion. Without it, the taste of enlightened hearers cannot be satisfied, and even the uncultivated, though they may not know why, will be far less deeply impressed. But unity in an expository discourse is by many preachers never aimed at.[49]

So, being intentional about unity in your exposition will contribute to a decisional emphasis. Lack of unity, on the other hand, will cause your listeners to lose interest and miss an encounter with the supernatural text.

Let your Text Determine Your Sermon Subject

If you expose the Holy Spirit's intended meaning in the text, then it follows naturally that your sermon subject will be about something God has addressed. The subject is the broad central thrust of the message and is typically reflected in the main idea of the sermon. We can find ideas for sermons just about anywhere. Sometimes we see them in human needs, or maybe situations that characterize our congregation as a whole, or possibly even within our own personal experience. While sermon ideas can arise from just about anywhere, that doesn't mean they should automatically become the subject of a sermon. Why? Because a sermon idea isn't necessarily equivalent to biblical truth! In other words, we have to make sure our sermon idea is actually a subject that God addresses in the Bible. That's what makes it legitimate—and supernatural—preaching material.

Beloved fellow preacher, always remember that you haven't been called to address every issue known to mankind. You've been called to proclaim God's truth as it's revealed in Scripture, largely because that's the only hope your listeners have of life transformation. Just because you have a sermon idea doesn't necessarily mean you have a preaching subject. Always take your sermon idea to the biblical text to see whether or not God talked about that subject in a definitive and direct way. If He did, then you have something to preach! The subjects God addresses in the Bible are the subjects that carry other-worldly power. To maximize decisional impact in your sermon, your subject needs to be dictated by the text of Scripture, not by your whims or those of your audience.

Sermons on scriptural subjects possess an intrinsic ability to affect hearers positively. George Sweazey says, "A more than worldly help is given to a sermon by its more than worldly subject matter."[50]

Biblical subjects offer a sublime appeal because God's promises are true. Even most people who reject the idea of supernatural power regard the Bible as possessing some special note of authority. So, let your particular biblical text dictate your sermon subject. A scriptural subject—born on the wings of the convicting power of the Holy Spirit—is the means by which people are called to repentance and faith in Christ, and then re-created into His image.

Highlight the Gospel in Your Text

Every text in the Bible stands somewhere in relation to the Gospel of Jesus Christ. Tony Merida contends, "Every text will point to Christ futuristically, refer to Christ explicitly, or look back to Christ implicitly."[51] And since the Gospel of Christ "is the power of God for salvation to everyone who believes" (Rom 1:16), identifying and proclaiming that relationship is one of the most important keys to exposing listeners to the spiritual muscle necessary for life change. You will greatly strengthen your decisional influence when you highlight the Gospel in every text and demonstrate how Jesus Christ is the feature of all biblical truth.

Gospel-centered emphasis provides the solid foundation on which spiritual decisions are made. This subject possesses unique power to move people. The good news about Christ possesses an innate quality that calls people to change and action. Why? Because it invites people to respond to a person, not an ideology. Charles Koller explains:

> In all Biblical preaching God seeks primarily, through His messenger, to bring man into fellowship with Himself. The aim, therefore, is not merely to impart knowledge, or provoke thought, or arouse the emotions, but to move

> the will to an affirmative response. And the response that saves the soul is always, of necessity, the response of a person to a Person. A valid, saving faith is not merely the acceptance of a "way of life," a philosophy, a principle, or a set of principles. It is the response of the creature to his Creator, the subject to his rightful Sovereign, the soul to the Savior.... This response to the risen Christ is the very password into the Kingdom of God. "By *me*, if any man enter in, he shall be saved . . ." John 10:9. . . . When Jesus was testing the faith of Peter, He did not say, "Peter, lovest thou my principles, my policies, my program"; but "lovest thou *me*?" (John 21:17).[52]

Gospel-centered preaching calls individuals to decide on a relationship with a person and not just a change of action.

As you highlight the Gospel connection in every message, be sure to appeal to unbelievers to trust in Christ. Taking time to do this even when you're primarily addressing believers in your sermon will foster a decisional emphasis in your preaching. It will not only refresh the hearts of your believing listeners, but it will generate spiritual power and create an atmosphere conducive for evangelistic fruit. Taking the time to briefly address subjects like the nature of salvation, how to experience salvation, the benefits of salvation, and the consequences of rejecting salvation are always beneficial for both believers and unbelievers. The Gospel confronts unbelievers with the need to decide for Christ, but it also refreshes and strengthens the faith of believers. D. Martyn Lloyd-Jones asserts that

> all the people who attend a church need to be brought under the power of the Gospel. The Gospel is not merely

and only for the intellect; and if our preaching is always expository and for edification and teaching it will produce church members who are hard and cold, and often harsh and self-satisfied.[53]

Gospel themes have decisional benefit for all listeners, and the neglect of including them in our preaching hinders spiritual growth.

SERMON FORM

As I've previously noted, rhetoric wasn't initially the imposition of some secular philosophy on the spiritual business of preaching. It was actually the systematization of persuasive, effective communication. So, by and large, rhetoric isn't an evil that preachers need to shun, but instead an asset we need to use to serve God's purpose in our preaching. Structure is one aspect of Christian sermons that was influenced by rhetorical thought throughout the first three centuries AD. While the traditional homily was common during that time, by the end of the third century preachers began to abandon it for more orderly structure and unifying themes.[54]

When we have a strong foundation that's focused on the biblical text and its Gospel centricity, we can now build a framework for our sermons that favors decision making. How you structure your sermon will affect its decisional quality. Broadus asserts that good structure makes every sermon more persuasive.[55] When I refer to sermon structure I'm referring to the major parts of the sermon and their subsequent arrangement. Often called *formal elements*, the major parts minimally include the introduction, the exposition (or body), and the conclusion. While there are many qualities of each of these three parts that can contribute to the call for decision, let me identify one in each area that provides particular decisional energy.

Propose to Your People in Your Introduction

Marriage proposals are much more involved than they used to be. Some guys hire photographers to hide in the bushes and take pictures of them as they pop the question as part of what appears to be a Hollywood production of events. Others pay big bucks to get down on one knee while a stadium full of spectators watch on the jumbotron at an athletic event. I wasn't that smart—or resourceful. I asked my wife to marry me sitting in a '67 Camaro in the parking lot of the Atlanta airport. Real romantic, huh? She came into town to visit me at one point during our long-distance relationship, and I couldn't wait any longer. Needless to say, the formalization of our journey didn't happen with a lot of fanfare.

Regardless of whether a guy asks for a girl's hand with a lot of hoopla or not, a proposal is a big deal. Asking someone to marry you is weighty business. You're asking a lady to come off the market, give up her life for you, be committed to you for the rest of your lives, and much more. That's no small ask! And what we want is for the girl to say "yes" to our proposal. I'm convinced that one of the biggest reasons many preachers fail to preach for decision is that they don't see people's response to God's Word as that big of a deal. They don't see it as having weighty, eternal consequences. If we believe the Gospel is a matter of life and death, then it merits our pleading with people to decide rightly for it.

That's why I like to use the word *proposition* to describe the big idea of the sermon. I think it reminds us that we're proposing to people to say "yes" to God's Word. Whether we're talking to believers or unbelievers, we want them to embrace the truth that we're preaching. That's why persuasive propositional statements enhance a preacher's decisional force. And in most cases the best place to include this statement is in the introduction of your sermon where it can reveal your intent, provide your listeners with a clear line of direction to what you're proposing they embrace, and point them to the place of conviction and decision. On the flip side, "a sermon without recognizable purpose and progression may lead to bewilderment rather than conviction and decision."[56]

A sermon is only as persuasive to an audience as it is connected with the audience. Decisional introductions with a clear proposition facilitate the kind of connection we want to make. While a sermon introduction doesn't contain any innate life-changing power, it's there that we buy the right to take our listeners on to the exposition of God's truth in the body of the sermon. Exposition, you'll remember, is the only part of the sermon that contains supernatural power for life change. But in order for listeners to encounter that life-changing component, we first have to get them to it. The purpose of the introduction is to do just that—to win their attention and gain their interest so they'll travel with us to our treatment of the biblical text. We want them to be drawn in, not turned away. We want them to think, "Hmm, I want to hear what the Bible has to say about this subject."

A key component of the introduction, then, should be a clear, heartfelt proposition that bottom-lines God's meaning in the text. It whets people's appetite for what God is going to say and establishes in their minds that they are being asked to decide about something. Robinson, whose name often is associated with the "big idea" in sermons, highlights the relationship between propositions and decision making:

> Effective sermons major in biblical ideas brought together into an overarching unity. Having thought God's thoughts after Him, the expositor communicates and applies those thoughts to his hearers. In dependence upon the Holy Spirit, he aims to confront, convict, convert, and comfort men and women through the preaching of biblical concepts. He knows people shape their lives and settle their eternal destinies in response to ideas.[57]

The proposition is the "big idea" of the sermon. It's a capsule of the truth about which people must decide. It's the biblical idea for which they must render a verdict. It's the proposal to which we want them to say "yes."

Effective propositions can be very persuasive. Sometimes your proposition will express a direct appeal to your audience. You might say something like, "In this text, you're going to hear God tell you to start loving the people who hate you." From the beginning of the message you're explicitly and candidly compelling your listeners to respond to the message that's to follow. At other times your proposition will persuade people by asserting that particular truths will lead to their benefit. You may propose something like, "Jesus invites you and me to get in His yoke where we can rest from trying to earn God's favor."

G. Campbell Morgan was a firm believer in the persuasive nature of propositions. In fact, he contends that a proposition needs to express or imply some kind of audience response toward which the sermon will be moving. Morgan believes this goal of response is implicit in preaching. He says, "A discourse which makes no spiritual or moral appeal or demand is not a sermon."[58] If the call for decision is implicit in true preaching, then why not put "the ask" on the table from the very outset of your sermon? Propose to your people in your introduction and compel them to say "yes" to it.

Escort Your People in Your Exposition

Just about every time I go overseas I have to have someone on the ground to escort me to where I'm going. I've flown into urban areas where there were masses of people and buildings, remote areas where there wasn't any electricity to see at night, wooded areas where there were wild animals roaming about, and hostile areas where there were people who didn't want me there. I'm always comforted and encouraged when someone meets me at the airport and escorts me to where I'm going. I frequently need someone who can not only accompany me on my journey, but someone who can speak the language and get me to where I'm going without getting into trouble.

My friend, Robert Smith, likens the preacher's job to that of an "exegetical escort."[59] He takes the idea from the apostle Paul when he said that "the law was our guardian" (Gal 3:24). The word translated *guardian* is *paidogogos*, which means "tutor" or "trainer." Smith says, "The Law served as a schoolmaster that escorted or ushered us to Christ. Preachers become, for the people in churches, escorts who take the Word and usher them into the presence of God as *paidogogos* for the purpose of transformation."[60] That's what we do when we expose the right meaning of the biblical text. We escort people into God's presence and let them hear His voice. And that voice transforms them.

The biblical text is a frightening place to a lot of people, even for those who have grown up in Christian contexts. Just reading and studying the Bible is a scary task for a whole lot of people, not to mention being asked to render a decision about its content. That's why one of the most important things you can do in your sermon is skillfully escort people through the biblical text in such a way that they safely arrive at the place of understanding just why God put that passage in the Bible. When you do so, you not only put their minds at ease by accompanying them on the trip, but you guide them to understand God's truth and protect them from misinterpreting it. A good escort knows the best route to the destination and how to avoid pitfalls along the way.

One of the most important ways to escort our listeners through our exposition—or sermon body—is to give them clear direction and handles on which to hold. To do that, we need to develop our exposition logically, using well-crafted and clearly articulated major divisions, or points. We often refer to this kind of structure as the "outline" of the sermon. Ideally, each division of the outline supports the sermon's proposition and summarizes its manageable development.[61] In other words, the outline provides a logical framework for unpacking the proposition. Listeners develop an affinity for the salient truth as it's communicated to them in manageable units. Without a clear, logical outline the sermon loses much of its power. With it, persuasiveness increases by providing intelligent guidance for reasonable action and appealing to the logical thought processes of the mind.

Logical arrangement, then, assists in creating decisional force. Good major headings provide the steps your listeners use to navigate the biblical text and understand the thrust of your message. And that understanding provides the impetus for decision. Just like the voice on your GPS tells you to "go 500 feet and then turn left," and then "in one mile use the right two lanes to exit right," the points of your outline provide clear steps to arrive at the intended destination—deciding rightly for God's truth. It's been said that the "preacher loves his hearers when he orders his sermons in a way that draws them to the truth, feeds their minds and hearts, and calls them to respond appropriately to the Word of God."[62] Like a good GPS and a faithful escort, guide your listeners through to the end.

Call Your People in Your Conclusion

The conclusion of your sermon brings your exposition to a proper end and calls your listeners to act on it. I love the way Broadus describes this part of the sermon as "a leave taking, in which [the preacher] commits vital and eternal issues to the decision of those who have heard him. He leaves the responsibility of action to them."[63] That's what you have to do when you conclude your message—leave the call for response in the laps of your listeners. The most effective—and neglected—way to leave this call with your people is to exhort them to respond. Exhortation, or direct appeal, is the dominant characteristic in the most compelling conclusions. One writer describes such appeal in the conclusion as "a challenge to respond, a call to do something specific in response to the message."[64]

One of the tragedies in our day is that so many preachers try to preach with dry eyes. We don't carry the burden of the prophet for people to hear and obey what God says. What Broadus said of his day is true of ours as well. Most preachers have "lost the unembarrassed urgency of importuning men for God" even though such appeals characterized prophetic and apostolic preaching.[65]

Exhorting people through direct appeals in the sermon conclusion reflects the decisional purpose of the sermon. People are encouraged to respond to the truth that is delivered. One of the things that has caused many preachers to avoid pleading with people is that they've seen many other preachers use manipulation and intimidation to try to force decisions as opposed to simply exhorting the congregation to respond to what's just been expounded.[66] But somebody else's dirty bathwater doesn't justify our throwing out the baby when we discard their water. Scripture compels us to exhort and plead and implore people to say "yes" to God's Word.

The way to avoid manipulation in your sermon conclusion is to do your job with your exposition. If you expounded the truth of the passage with integrity, then you're on safe ground in making direct and emotional appeals in your conclusion. Why? Because you're pleading with people based on truth, not on emotions. You may appeal to their emotions, but your appeal is based on truth. Manipulation happens when we appeal to people based upon something other than truth. Solid content in your exposition enhances the effectiveness of emotional appeals in your conclusion.

When you plead with people based on truth, it's entirely proper to express feeling and emotion when exhorting people to respond. Remember, emotion and emotionalism are two different things. Emotions are God given and should be used to express a God-given burden for our listeners. In turn, our listeners' emotions should be one of the targets of our appeals. You have the freedom and responsibility to conclude your sermons with passionate appeals for people to make decisions. Don't leave any room for your people to doubt your desire for them to respond rightly. So call them to do so with all of your heart!

SUMMARY

I ended the last chapter by looking into the necessity of the Spirit's attendance to our preaching. We need His presence and power if we're to expect biblical application and life transformation in our listeners. Remember, the Spirit of God is the author of the Word of God (2 Pet 1:19-21; 2 Tim 3:16), and the Word of God is the testimony of the Son of God (Luke 24:27; John 5:39). Furthermore, the Spirit of God is called the Spirit of Truth and the Spirit of Christ (John 14:17; Rom 8:9). The closer our sermons are tied to the Word of God and the Son of the God, the more potential they have to be anointed by the presence and power of the Spirit of God. Words abound in sermons all around, but power doesn't. "For the kingdom of God does not consist in talk but in power" (1 Cor 4:20). Let's allow the text to drive both the meaning and message of our sermons as we highlight Christ and His Gospel. In doing so, perhaps we and our listeners will indeed experience the true kingdom of God through our preaching.

Please understand that I'm not talking about calling people to respond with some immediate, public expression of their decision like an altar call. We'll tackle that issue a bit later. I'm not even talking about limiting your call for decision to your conclusion. I'm talking about your responsibility to call your listeners to act on the message of the text throughout your sermon. You don't preach to hear yourself talk or to give people Bible facts. You preach for changed lives, so you're calling for a verdict. The conclusion is your last opportunity to specifically and formally call for that verdict, but you should be doing that in your introduction and exposition as well. So look for ways to appeal to your people all the through your sermon, and then finish with a passionate exhortation for them to obey what they've heard.

CHAPTER IV

DECISIONAL QUALITIES OF SERMON FUNCTION

In addition to turning me on to the term *decisional preaching*, Chuck Kelley at New Orleans Seminary also helped me learn how to be intentional about what I let into my sermons. And his help came—of all places—through some advice he gave me as I was preparing to write my dissertation! He told me to get two folders, one labeled "Dissertation" and another labeled "Good Stuff." He said I would need them when I started researching my subject in the library because I was going to dig up all kinds of interesting information, some of which wouldn't need to find its way into my dissertation. So he told me that whenever I found something related to my topic, I needed to ask the question as to whether it helped me prove my thesis. "If it does," he said, "put it in the 'Dissertation' folder and use it in your report. If it doesn't, then put it in the 'Good Stuff' folder and come back to it later and use it at some other time in your ministry." He finished with a stern warning: "But whatever you do, don't let it in your dissertation if it doesn't help you prove your thesis!"[67]

That's good advice—not only for writing a dissertation—but also for building decisional sermons. Everything in your sermon needs to have function, a reason for being there. You determine what needs to be there by whether or not it helps you get people to your proposition—your thesis—so your audience can say "yes" to it. So for every bit of your exegetical information you need to ask whether it helps you prove your proposition convincingly. If it does, then include it. If it doesn't, then file it away for use at another time. But whatever you do, don't let it in your sermon if it doesn't help you prove your proposition!

For all the material that makes the cut, organize it by the purpose it's going to fulfill—or the role it's going to play—in your message. Normally, we categorize sermonic information by one of four functions: explanation, application, illustration, and argumentation. These are known as the *functional elements* in preaching. Regarding your proposition, you need to ask: 1) What needs to be explained? 2) What needs to be applied? 3) What needs to be illustrated? and 4) What needs to be argued? The answers to those questions should determine what you let in your sermon. While there are multiple decisional qualities for each of these four functional elements, let me offer one potent challenge that relates to the major purpose of each one.

Explain to Transform

Explanation is the functional element we use to make biblical information understandable. But that's not end game. We don't explain information that we dig up in our Bible study just so people can understand biblical facts better. We explain it so they can understand it because that's what changes them! We're often led to believe that application is what brings about life change. Application doesn't change people; it just helps them demonstrate the change that's already taken place inside them. We'll talk more about that idea later. Bill Hull says, "Transformation comes through the commitment of the mind. Without the proper knowledge and thinking we have no basis for personal change or growth. The mind is the pivotal starting place for change."[68] So we explain the meaning of a Bible text so that people can understand it and be transformed by it.

Explaining for transformation is at the heart of the biblical model for preaching. In Nehemiah 8:1-12, some form of the word "understand" is used five times in the first twelve verses (see Neh 8:2-3, 7-8, 12). This emphasis is capsulized in the summary statement that the Levites "read from the book, from the Law of God, clearly, and they gave the sense, so that the people understood the reading" (Neh 8: 8). The word "clearly" means to distinguish, or to specify distinctly. The word "sense" means to give the meaning, indicating perception or insight. They broke the Scriptures down into manageable parts in order to make it understandable.

Similarly, Jesus provided clear explanation to His hearers, both in the synagogue worship and in other contexts. He often read and explained the Scriptures as a visiting rabbi (cf. Luke 4:16-21). To the disciples on the Emmaus road, "beginning at Moses and all the Prophets, he interpreted to them in all the Scriptures the things concerning himself" (Luke 24: 27). The word translated "interpreted" means to unfold the meaning or to explain through. Reflecting on His teaching, those disciples asked, "Did not our hearts burn within us while he talked with us on the road, while He opened to us the Scriptures?" (Luke 24: 32). The word "opened" means to open thoroughly. He opened the sense of the Scriptures by explaining them.[69]

Other New Testament preachers also were intentional about explaining what was obscure and hard to understand (cf. Mark 4:34;

Acts 9:29; 2 Pet 1:20). In Thessalonica, the Apostle Paul was "explaining and proving that it was necessary for the Christ to suffer and to rise from the dead" (Acts 17:2–3). He instructed Timothy, "Until I come, devote yourself to the public reading of Scripture, to exhortation, to teaching" (1 Tim 4:13). He told him that if he didn't do anything else, he needed to read the Scripture to people, explain it to them, and implore them to say "yes" to it. Bible preachers explained God's Word to people so they could understand it and be changed by it.

So, in a very real sense, explanation is the most crucial functional element for life change. All the other elements serve it in some way. We don't just do application; we apply biblical truth rightly understood through explanation. We don't just use illustrations in our sermons; we use them to clarify biblical truth and apply it rightly. We don't just engage in argumentation when we preach; we argue against assertions in our listeners' minds that are contrary to biblical truth so they will understand and embrace what God says.

One of the distinctive characteristics of expository preaching is its instructional function. The explanation of details in a text imparts information that is otherwise unavailable to untrained listeners. This information provides listeners with a foundation for growth and service.[70] So we explain the significance of words and phrases in discourses as well as interpret actions and events embedded within narrative material. Sometimes this requires dividing the text into words, phrases, and ideas, and then explaining the components in understandable terms. At other times it involves explaining certain subjects related to a text. On occasion it requires explaining nuances in the original languages. When you do this, however, be sure not to flaunt your knowledge of the biblical languages, but instead to simply use your ability to provide adequate explanation.

Remember, we're not talking about explaining everything in your text. We're talking about explaining only the details that are necessary to clarify the proposition for your preaching passage, so be selective about what you explain. Preaching isn't loading up a dump truck with exegetical data, backing it up to your congregation, and dumping it on them. Be intentional about what you give them. And what you give them, give them in a way that suits their vocabulary and context. You need to convey in the language of a non-specialist what you learned from specialized analysis. Robert L. Thomas says this skill is at "the core of Bible exposition."[71]

Explaining for transformation is crucial in the relationship between the listeners' understanding of truth and their subsequent decision for it. Stott asserts that the great doctrines of the Bible imply that man has an inescapable obligation both to think and act on what he thought and knew.[72] Preacher, explain the Bible to your people so they can be transformed by it.

Argue to Convince

Just because you explain your biblical text well doesn't mean everyone who hears you will believe what you say. The day is long gone in which people believe something just because the Bible and the preacher say it. I'm thankful we live in a day in which biblical exposition is on the rise and people are being helped to know more about what the Bible actually says and means. But just because they understand it doesn't mean they automatically believe it. If I explain and proclaim, "Love your neighbor," most people will understand it and believe it. But if I explain and declare, "Jesus is the only way to heaven," everybody may understand it, but a sizeable number of them won't necessarily agree with it. As our culture becomes more characterized by secularism, pluralism, relativism, and biblical illiteracy, preachers are going to have to become more skilled in the art of argumentation.[73]

When we talk about argumentation in preaching, we're simply referring to the act of persuading with the intent of changing an attitude or action. Argumentation involves the use of reason, discussion, and dispute. It contributes to a decisional emphasis in preaching because its goal is to persuade someone to change an attitude or an action. We want them to change their position—or conviction—about something. We want them to be convinced of the biblical view.

The Apostle Paul apparently took this element of preaching and teaching the Scriptures seriously. The Acts narrative is especially replete with references to his sanctified arguments with people he was trying to 'convince' about the Gospel. Notice the frequency of the words *reason* and *persuade*:

> And Paul went in, as was his custom, and on three Sabbath days he *reasoned* with them from the Scriptures. (Acts 17:2; emphasis mine)

> So he *reasoned* in the synagogue with the Jews and the devout persons, and in the marketplace every day with those who happened to be there. (Acts 17:17; emphasis mine)

> And he *reasoned* in the synagogue every Sabbath, and tried to *persuade* Jews and Greeks. (Acts 18:4; emphasis mine)

> And they came to Ephesus, and he left them there, but he himself went into the synagogue and *reasoned* with the Jews. (Acts 18:19; emphasis mine)

> And he entered the synagogue and for three months spoke boldly, *reasoning* and *persuading* them about the kingdom of God. But when some became stubborn and continued in unbelief, speaking evil of the Way before the congregation, he withdrew from them and took the disciples with him, *reasoning* daily in the hall of Tyrannus. (Acts 19:8–9; emphasis mine)

> And as he *reasoned* about righteousness and self-control and the coming judgment, Felix was alarmed and said, "Go away for the present. When I get an opportunity I will summon you." (Acts 24:25; emphasis mine)

The focus of argumentation is actually the use of reason and discussion in order to convince someone of a particular position and persuade them to embrace it.[74] And Paul employed it regularly in his efforts to get people to decide rightly for the Gospel.

As much as understanding what argumentation is, it's also important to understand what it's not. It's not proving the listener's position to be false and the biblical position to be true *beyond any shadow of a doubt*. A defense lawyer in a court of law doesn't have to prove his case beyond refute. He needs only to establish reasonable doubt in the minds of the jurors. Similarly, when you're defending the faith in the preaching event, you don't have to prove your point beyond rebuttal. All you have to do is bring your listeners to the place of at least entertaining the possibility that the biblical position could be valid. That creates the fertile soil in which the Holy Spirit does His convincing work.[75]

Although the nature of argumentation is reason and discussion, it's hard for many people to break away from the familiar connotations of controversy and dispute. Because the word *argue* frequently is associated with contention and unfriendly debate, we tend to neglect this aspect of decisional preaching. Most people don't like confrontation and do everything they can to stay away from it. It's part of human nature. Most of us preachers aren't any different. So we tend to give our time to explaining the text, illustrating it, and applying it. But we avoid argumentation like the plague! Broadus suggests this has been characteristic of public speakers throughout history:

> There are preachers, it is true, who seem to consider that they have no occasion for reasoning, that everything is to be accomplished by authoritative assertion and impassioned appeal. And this notion is not new; for we find Aristotle complaining that previous writers on Rhetoric had concerned themselves only with the means of persuasion by appeals to feeling and prejudice.[76]

Argumentation has an obvious and direct relationship with the call for decision, so you need to consciously take advantage of its decisional benefit in your sermons. If you want people to decide rightly for Gospel truth, times will come when you'll need to argue a point with intelligent reasoning.

Therein is one of the major differences between explanation and argumentation. While most of the material you'll need to explain in a sermon will come from your exegetical material, what you argue will most often need to be developed by logical reasoning. John Calvin and Charles Finney—both of whom were trained in law before they began to preach—used argumentation effectively in their preaching. The Apostle Paul—having been schooled in ancient oratory and rhetoric—skillfully used the art of argumentation in his preaching as well. That doesn't mean, however, that you need formal training to argue certain positions in your sermons. You simply need to ask God for a keen sense of discernment, intentionally identify issues in your preaching text that might hinder the audience from embracing your proposition, and then discuss them in a logical fashion in the spirit of Christ.

One of the most important tasks in argumentation, then, is learning to anticipate the objections listeners may have to the truths you'll be presenting. To determine what aspects of the passage need to be argued, ask the following question of all the exegetical information you've determined to be necessary to prove your proposition: *What assertion(s) won't my audience immediately agree with?* As you ask this question, don't raise objections that your listeners are not likely to raise! And whatever you do, pray for God's grace to show respect and consideration for those who may hold positions contrary to the biblical position for which you intend to argue.[77]

While there are many ways to argue a position, one of the most important for decisional preaching is called "refutation," or rebuttal. You can heighten decisional impact by directly refuting objections to biblical truth. Refutation involves tactfully and diplomatically showing an objection to be erroneous or false. You can't afford to be afraid to refute the perceived erroneous reasoning of your listeners. While our tendency would be to think that refutation would be contrary to moving people toward rightly deciding for Gospel truth, actually the opposite is the case. While most people don't go looking for conflict, they do admire and sympathize with someone who appears to be "a fearless defender of unpopular doctrines."[78] But we have to do it with the right attitude. Alexander Vinet warns, "We are more inclined to refute than to prove, to destroy than to build up. It is more easy, more flattering to self-love, more in accordance with our natural passions. Everyone is eloquent in anger; love and peace seldom make men eloquent."[79] In other words, we better argue in the Spirit and not in the flesh!

With God's help you can strike a balance in argumentation by seizing the natural magnetism of refutation without alienating listeners. Consider introducing an argument you're about to make by saying something like "You say," "Someone may say," or "People say." This approach couches your argument in a dialogue with your listeners. As you prepare your sermon and anticipate a possible objection, imagine yourself in the place of the listeners. Then raise issues in your mind that you think the audience might raise during the sermon. This exercise prepares you for their skepticism and helps you to prepare to dialogue with them instead of sounding like you're hating on them.

A while back I was preaching from Hebrews 10:24–25. As I prepared, I knew I wanted to make some application regarding the importance of us being faithful to gather together regularly as a faith community. In my study I began to anticipate excuses that some listeners make for not being consistent in church attendance. One of the objections I identified was that some adults contend they don't come to church regularly because they were always made to go when they were growing up. So, at the appropriate spot in my sermon, I said,

> Some of you are saying, "I don't like to come to church because my parents forced me to go all the time as a child." And I get that, because I was made to do a lot of things when I was growing up as well. But let me ask you something today: Do you brush your teeth regularly? I would venture to say that most—if not all—of you would answer that question with a "yes." But I would also venture to say that most of us had to be hounded by our parents to brush our teeth consistently. As kids, that wasn't something most of us really enjoyed doing. But yet we do it as adults. Why? Because, along the way, we learned that it's good

for us. So, there actually are some things we were forced to do as children that we now do as adults because we've learned they're good for us. The author of Hebrews, under the inspiration of the Holy Spirit tells us that gathering together regularly as believers is good for us.

Now, I didn't prove my point beyond any shadow of a doubt or possibility of rebuttal. But by couching my argument in dialogue, I did at least open the door for my listeners to entertain the idea that coming to church regularly might be good for them. And prayerfully, they will decide accordingly.

Beloved, let me encourage you to use this dialogical approach and other methods of arguing biblical positions in your sermons. Work hard at anticipating audience objections in advance through the use of mock dialogue and allow the Holy Spirit to use it to encourage decisions to Gospel truth.

Apply to Demonstrate

Even when we explain biblical truth to people, convince them to embrace it, and watch God do His transforming work in their lives, we're still not done. We still must help them live out their transformation through obedience. And we do that through the functional element of application. Application involves relating the sermon to your audience, involving them in its subject, and calling them to act on its challenge.

But contrary to popular understanding, we do application as a *demonstration* of spiritual transformation, not as a *means* to it. To be sure, a lot of so-called expository preaching has been characterized by an overload of exegetical details with no connection to the real world.

That's not expository preaching; that's *poor* expository preaching. The goal of true expository preaching must be to secure some moral action, not simply to communicate doctrine. A. W. Tozer reminds us that "there is scarcely anything so dull and meaningless as Bible doctrine taught for its own sake. Truth divorced from life is not truth in its Biblical sense, but something else and something less. . . . Theological truth is useless until it is obeyed."[80]

Today, however, it seems that scenario often is reversed. Many guys are preaching more application at the expense of needed exegetical details of the text. Doing so not only misses the nature of true application, but it undermines and nullifies the possibility of real life change.

Preachers must make application in their sermons through the right lens. Application doesn't cause transformation; it simply gives transformation the opportunity to be demonstrated. The Apostle Paul describes this relationship when he says,

> I appeal to you therefore, brothers, by the mercies of God, to present your bodies as a living sacrifice, holy and acceptable to God, which is your spiritual worship. ²Do not be conformed to this world, but be transformed by the renewal of your mind, that by testing you may discern what is the will of God, what is good and acceptable and perfect. (Rom 12:1–2)

The appeal *to present your bodies* is an obvious call to sacrificially live something out, or practice it. But how do you do that? You do it by being "transformed by the renewal of your mind." The Word of God, rightly explained and understood, serves as the primary agent of transforming our thinking, which then leads to the transformation of our acting.

But Paul isn't done. The word translated "discern" means to 'test and prove' or 'approve as a result of testing.' Approve what? "The will of God." Living out God's truth (application) is the demonstration and validation of real spiritual transformation that has taken place as a result of saying "yes" to God's Word. His Word acts as the objective revelation of His will, and our obedience to it confirms that we've genuinely embraced it. When we discover that God's will is "good and acceptable and perfect," then we're responsible for putting it into practice.[81] Stott summarizes this whole process: "Here then are the stages of Christian moral transformation: first our mind is renewed by the Word and Spirit of God; then we are able to discern and desire the will of God; and then we are increasingly transformed by it."[82]

Life change doesn't take place from the outside-in, but from the inside-out. God changes us through His Word, and then we live out that change in our behavior. Application implies an object—something has to be applied. That something is the truth rightly explained and understood. The truth of Scripture is the only object that fosters change when applied to listeners. Consequently, that's the preacher's job. We need to show how the truth can be fleshed out in the lives of our people. Thomas writes:

> Such a service is the ideal way to cooperate with the Holy Spirit who inspired Scripture as He takes an improved grasp of the text's meaning and shows its applicational significance to individual listeners. This is the best avenue for building up the saints. The New Testament puts heavy emphasis on using the mind as the principal avenue to Christian growth.[83]

Thompson is even more specific, saying that in every sermon "listeners are enabled to see how their world, like the biblical world, is addressed by the word of God and are enabled to respond to that word."[84]

Consequently, fellow preacher, you don't have to live under the pressure of making good application in your sermons so people will be changed. But you do have the responsibility of giving them some ways to demonstrate the change that God's supernatural Word—rightly understood—has brought about in them. So explanation and application are partners. We explain the truth to give understanding and allow God to bring about life change. We apply the truth to provide indication of relevance for the listeners so they can flesh it out.

I realize there are numerous ways to do application and to help foster healthy demonstration of spiritual decisions. Let me offer three that I think are especially potent and yet often overlooked. First, exhort your people. Sometimes we forget that exhortation is actually application. Whenever you make a direct appeal to your people to say "yes" to biblical truth, you're applying truth to their lives. Pleading with people to embrace spiritual truth that you've explained not only maintains a direct relationship between application and explanation, but it also motivates people to positive action. They know exactly what they're being asked to do. The entire content of your message should be such that the listeners will understand the truth more clearly and be persuaded to accept it. So plead with them to decide rightly for it.

Second, challenge your people to *believe* stuff, not just *do* stuff. I know this sounds strange because we most often think of application as *doing* something. But what we do in life is based on what we believe. Application is as much about helping people decide to believe rightly as it is helping them to decide to act rightly. An old extrabiblical proverb says, "If you give a man a fish, you feed him for a day. If you teach a man to fish, you feed him for a lifetime." When we challenge people to say "yes" to the great doctrines of the Bible—to good and right theology—we're shaping in them a worldview that will determine decisions they make and behavior they demonstrate every day of the rest of their lives. Preacher, teach your people to fish by challenging them to believe Gospel truth rightly!

Third, make much of the cross and the crucified life. The Apostle Paul said, "I decided to know nothing among you except Jesus Christ and him crucified" (1 Cor 2:2). I don't think he was saying in that claim that all he did was give some version of the "Four Spiritual Laws" or the "Romans Road" every week. He wasn't saying all he did was preach salvation messages. He was articulating his understanding that the cross was not only the way we're justified, but it's the way we're sanctified as well. Paul got this conviction from Jesus. Our Lord had taught His disciples, "If anyone would come after me, let him deny himself and take up his cross daily and follow me. For whoever would save his life will lose it, but whoever loses his life for my sake will save it" (Luke 9:23–24). Paul resolved to preach the cross to both unbelievers and believers because he knew it was the key to the entire journey of salvation.

Based on Jesus's teaching, Paul knew the cross was the message of salvation for unbelievers, but he also knew that believers would need to revisit the cross *every day*! He later would write that he counted all his accomplishments as nothing to the end "that I may know him and the power of his resurrection, and may share his sufferings, becoming like him in his death, that by any means possible I may attain the resurrection from the dead" (Phil 3:10–11). He believed the crucified life was the way for him to know Christ more and to be shaped into His image. His words in Romans 12:1–2 discussed above also reflect his conviction that we must regularly die on the altar of the crucified life as an expression of our worship and that in so doing we will demonstrate God's "good and acceptable and perfect" will. Preach the cross every time, and implore your people to die to self.

Illustrate to Clarify

I came to know Christ through an illustration. Weird, huh? I'm fully aware that the Gospel is God's power for salvation, and so I know that it was the Gospel that actually saved me. But I got to the Gospel through an illustration. I was raised in a wonderful Christian home by godly parents. But, as a nine-year-old boy, it would be a stretch to say that I was looking for God. But one Sunday night in a little country church in Alabama, I heard a story. I was sitting on the back row with my buddies, not paying any attention to the sermon. I was writing on the bulletin and flipping through the hymn book making fun of names like Fanny J. Crosby. Toward the end of the sermon my pastor started telling a story about a guy who kept saying "no" to God until it was too late. As he told that story, I sat up and listened. And my pastor used that story to lead into my need for the Gospel. That's how I got saved—through an illustration.

Illustrations are used to illuminate some aspect of the other three functional elements. The verb form, *illustrate*, comes from a Latin word that means "to cast light upon."[85] When used well, illustrations can cast light on explanation, application, and argumentation in such a way so as to intensify their decisional impact. In other words, it clarifies aspects of those other elements that are unfamiliar, cloudy, or a bit veiled so we can see them for what they really are. So, an illustration might clarify the meaning of a textual detail so we can understand it (explanation). An illustration might also cast some light on a certain truth so we know how to obey it (application). Or an illustration might illuminate our minds to a new way of thinking so that we change our position (argumentation).

The decisional value of an illustration, therefore, is discovered in its relationship to one of the other functional elements. In other words, illustrations serve the other functions and help them to accomplish their decisional impact. We don't just use illustrations in our sermons; we use illustrations for *something*, for some purpose, to accomplish some function. So, illustrations aren't an end in and of themselves. They are servants and, therefore, should always be used intentionally to help other elements in the sermon realize their decisional capacity to the greatest degree.

The most basic service that illustrations provide is clarification. The necessity of understanding in decision making that I addressed above raises the decisional value of using illustrations for this purpose. "Tangible representations and analogies help the congregation understand . . . and it is often the illustration that makes the listeners see what the minister is trying to say."[86] Since genuine decisions are contingent upon understanding, and illustrations enhance understanding, illustrations influence decision making in significant ways. They help us clarify the logic and reason of sermon ideas so listeners can decide rightly for them. Our work as preachers essentially "is to make men first see things, then feel them, then act upon them. If the first result is not gained the others will fail, while often if the first is gained, the other two will go."[87] Illustrations help people to see and feel so they can act.

In decisional preaching, certain kinds of illustrations often pack a bigger clarifying punch than others, such as illustrations that are both *familiar* and *frequented*. That's why Jesus used things like a sower and his seed, a vineyard, a yoke, and a fig tree. He knew that people were familiar with those things and that they likely would see them on the way home from His sermon and be reminded about the truth He had just taught. He used what people knew to interpret what they didn't know so they would be influenced to embrace it long after the sermon was over.[88]

So, let me challenge you to use ideas, concepts, and objects that are *familiar* to your people. When you use an illustration that involves something with which your listeners are familiar, they're more likely to understand what you're trying to say because they have some knowledge of it. Correspondingly, use things that will be *frequented* by your people after the sermon is over. Contrary to the phenomenal—almost unbelievable—stories that we often think make the best illustrations, the simple things that are common to everyday life usually pack the most lasting punch. And that's why everyday items like a vacuum cleaner, a car, a smartphone, or a computer will prove to be the most influential illustrations. Your people are familiar with these things, and they likely will encounter them after your sermon and be reminded of the scriptural truth that was illustrated.[89]

Just to give you an example, some time ago I used the autocorrect feature on my smartphone to illustrate God's help in suffering throughout a sermon from Romans 3:26-30. I opened up by telling the story about trying to send a text message to my wife that said, "I will love you forever." But because I mistakenly typed an "e" instead of an "o" in the word "love," the message was autocorrected to read, "I will leave you forever." I told them I had some damage control to do when I got home that evening! Needless to say, just about everyone in my audience could identify with that scenario. That kind of thing happens because my smartphone can't read my mind.

But then I told them that God had built an autocorrect feature into their suffering, and His autocorrect feature was always accurate and always on time. Then I expounded from the Romans 8 passage how God's sovereign hand and praying Spirit always have our backs. Even when we—or life in general—type in the wrong information that leaves us in desperate need of some damage control, God is always taking the good and bad that comes our way and turning it for the good of accomplishing His purpose of re-creation into Christ's image. The autocorrect feature on a computer, tablet, or smartphone isn't profound. But it's something with which most people in my audience were familiar, and one they likely used frequently in the days following the sermon.

Another effective kind of illustration that brings clarification and affects decision making is a narrative, or a story. My own testimony indicates the ability of short stories, parables, anecdotes, and vignettes to draw people of all ages in to an encounter with Gospel truth. If you're creative, you might use narratives that are born out of your own imagination. If you're like many of the rest of us, you might need to borrow from the narrative prowess of others.

Narrative illustrations can help convict people and make them aware of their need to act. This happens when we enable them to identify with some character or situation in a story. They see their sin, personal need, or lostness when they become involved in the story that somehow relates to their lives. When they see themselves in the story, then they make an appropriate response. Jesus, of course, used this approach frequently. Edgar Jackson observes:

> Jesus was a master at the devices of direct appeal to the attention and response of his listeners. . . . He used stories that were related to the experience of his hearers, and each story had one main point that stood out too clearly to be mistaken. The listener's interest is guaranteed by a plentiful use of narrative material. Not only does this serve the purpose of keeping the interest, but it also serves a more important psychological purpose of making it possible for

the hearer to identify himself with the characters of the story and live himself through the incidents.[90]

Jesus demonstrated how narrative illustrations directly appeal to the response of the hearers by enabling them to identify with the message. One author says, "The greatest convincer preached with stories."[91]

The nature of narrative also possesses decisional force because of its ability to seize and maintain the attention of all kinds of listeners. God has somehow wired the young and the old to be drawn to stories. Children love for their parents to read them bedtime stories. My aging mother-in-law lives with us, and her favorite pastime is to share stories of her childhood, as well as to trade them with those of other senior adults in her generation. Adams is right in that "it hardly matters what age one is; so long as he can understand what is said, he will give rapt attention and almost immediate response to a well-told story. Persons with the most diverse interests and backgrounds will perk up when they are about to be treated to a story."[92]

Let's just admit it—story form appeals to all of us, and it stirs something inside of us. Davis agrees regarding its influential quality:

> We underestimate the power of a narrative to communicate meaning and influence the lives of our people. We do it in spite of the obvious power of the myths, legends, and epics of mankind, and the tremendous influence which the novel and the drama--on stage, screen, radio, and television--have in shaping the opinions, the ethical ideas, and the behavior of the very people to whom we preach. No assertion about life has as much power as life itself has when shown to people.[93]

It was enough to break this young boy away from piddling with bulletins and songbooks long enough to encounter the Gospel. Today, it's enough to keep this grown man watching movies like *Remember the Titans* and the same episodes of *Person of Interest* over and over and over again. Go figure. Narrative grips us all.

One final—yet often neglected—kind of illustration that helps to clarify spiritual truth and foster decisional impact is the biblical illustration. Illustrations taken from the Bible—including stories, quotes, and examples—possess a unique ability to influence people toward spiritual decisions, yet they're often sacrificed for the pursuit of contemporary stories that are perceived to be more relevant. It would serve our preaching well, however, to turn more often to Scripture for illustrations because of their special ability to shed light on the great themes of our faith.

Implicitly, biblical illustrations possess two qualities that no other kind of illustration can claim. One, they possess a supernatural quality as part of inspired Scripture that's not characteristic of extrabiblical material. Two, they naturally address biblical illiteracy by educating listeners with more Bible knowledge. Emphasizing these decisional values, MacArthur states:

> Illustrations make an exposition *motivating*. Giving examples (especially biblical ones) of people whose experience illustrates a biblical principle will motivate hearers to put it into practice in their own lives. I look primarily for biblical illustrations. . . . Biblical illustrations, unlike non-biblical ones, have authority. Illustrations from other sources may be interesting and help hearers grasp a point better, but they are not the inspired Word of God. . . . They expand your people's knowledge of the Bible.[94]

With illustrations from the Bible, the listener's motivation to respond is influenced by both the power of Scripture and greater knowledge about the Bible.

Biblical illustrations are particularly helpful in fostering decision-making among believers. In fact, Broadus feels they're the best illustrations to use partly because the biblical material is somewhat familiar to most people in churches. Therefore, he concludes that they're readily intelligible.[95] Hall and Heflin agree: "The fact that they are often well known does not diminish their impact. . . . Use of biblical material strikes a responsive note, even though it is familiar."[96] Because most believers are familiar with so many Bible stories, verses, quotations, and doctrine, our exposition often comes alive in a special way when supported by such material. As the minds of believers are illuminated, they're more compelled to yield their lives to Bible truth.

SUMMARY

You can't afford not to be purposeful in sermons today. The Gospel is urgent. Time is short. People are passive. And just about every preaching context you have will have time limitations on it. There needs to be a reason for everything that's in your sermon, so make sure everything you say has a function. And make sure that function is serving the main idea of your text. Use what you say to unleash God's Word so it can do its transforming work in the lives of your people.

CHAPTER V

DECISIONAL QUALITIES OF SERMON FORCE

When people find out what I do as a vocation, it's not uncommon for them to ask in a bewildered tone, "How do you *teach* preaching?" It's a legitimate question. How do you teach something that's the result of God's call and takes the Holy Spirit to empower? My response is always the same. I tell people that my job isn't to teach guys to be polished orators, as if they could help the Gospel out by the way they speak. My job is to teach guys how to stay out of the way so the Gospel can do its work. We can't do anything to make the Word of God more powerful. We can, however, distract from it so that its power is veiled.

The Apostle Paul understood that it's possible for God's human instruments to get in the way of the message He calls them to proclaim. He told the Corinthians, "And I, when I came to you, brothers, did not come proclaiming to you the testimony of God with lofty speech or wisdom" (2 Cor 2:1). Paul wasn't saying that he came without any speech or wisdom. Certainly he had a good measure of both. The key to understanding his claim is in the little adjective *lofty*. It's a word than means "to rise above and reign supreme over." Paul understood that it's possible for our presentation of the truth to actually rise above the truth. We can present the right message, but present that message in such a way that we sidetrack it rather than serve it.

My experience has led me to believe that the most distracting element of preaching style is lack of force. I listen to a lot of preaching. Like other believers, I listen to preachers in churches, via podcasts, over the Internet, and on radio and TV. In addition to those venues, I listen to multiple students preach multiple times every semester as part of their ministry-training programs at our seminary. And without question the most glaring and most common deficiency is the lack of preaching force. Nothing is more distracting. Nothing veils the Gospel more. Nothing tempers the Spirit's power more. Nothing undermines more the supernatural ability of God's Word to effect life change. If we want to see people decide rightly for God's truth, then we have to understand sermon force and learn how to unleash it in our preaching.

UNDERSTANDING FORCE

All of us have heard people say things like, "Don't be so forceful!" or "Don't force your way in." Most of the time those exhortations are in response to a negative character quality or overbearing personality. That's why it's very important—from the outset of thinking about this subject—that we know what force is *not*. Force is not screaming, yelling, and slinging sweat. It's not running all over the platform when you preach. Force is not berating your audience and lording your authority over them, reminding them often of biblical excerpts like "touch not the Lord's anointed." Force is not pounding the pulpit every time you make a point (usually a weak one!). Just like our analysis of mysterious concepts like "the anointing" and "the filling of the Spirit," we tend to develop stereotypes of what force looks like.

In preaching, force is a positive thing. In fact, it's an indispensable element if preaching is to result in life change. Force—or energy—is the impact created by a combination of other elements of sermon style. It's the quality of propelling your thoughts into the hearts and minds of your listeners. Consequently, it normally provides more decisional influence than any other element of style. "It moves to action. It uses materials, language, and ideas to create a pressure toward accepting or acting in accord with the preacher's recommendations."[97] Force involves the energetic delivery that wins a response from the audience.

Another myth about preaching force is that it's limited to those preachers who have a strong or overbearing personality. Some preachers—for whom energetic thought and feeling don't come naturally—dismiss the responsibility of considering force in their preaching. They just claim to have a "get-out-of-jail-free-card" when it comes to force. So they give themselves a license to deliver lifeless and lackluster sermons every time they preach. At the same time, some preachers who do have stronger personalities think that means their sermons will automatically be forceful. Consequently, they allow their personalities to go unharnessed in their preaching and end up manifesting some of the misconceived ideas about force that I mentioned above. They forget that one of the secrets to great preaching is the preacher's willingness to die in the preaching event. Only then can his style—including his natural force—develop out of a redeemed personality.

Don't get me wrong. Certainly, a guy's naturally energetic personality can positively inform force in his preaching if it's channeled properly. Because energy naturally coexists with character, it surely can be manifested in speaking style through the personality of the preacher. Additionally, that mysterious chemistry created by the wedding of a particular personality with that of a congregation often creates a forceful dynamic. A great deal of some pastors' influence is due to the electricity that flows between them and their congregations. But when it comes to possessing effectual preaching force, the natural personality and congregational chemistry are the exceptions and not the rule. Even though those elements can be influential, the presence of force isn't dependent on them.

At the same time, force cannot be learned mechanically. In other words—like most elements of style—there's no magical formula that will produce preaching force if and when we check off all the right boxes. In fact, we likely have already discussed the primary influence on preaching force back in chapter 2 when dealing with the indispensable filling of the Spirit in the preaching event. That's the kind of force you can't do without. But while we can't go through a checklist, we can look at forceful preaching that affects life transformation and thus identify common denominators that seem to be frequently present. Then we can—and should—align ourselves with those elements. So let's consider how force is expressed in our preaching.

EXPRESSING FORCE

Force is just one of a number of elements of preaching style. Other elements include things like clarity, simplicity, and beauty. The presence or absence of these elements form the preacher's characteristic manner of expressing himself. Your style is the way you say things and do things when you're preaching. Style is at play in the words we use, how we use them, and the way we present them. Style is manifested both verbally and non-verbally. Like the other subjects I've discussed, there are multiple ways to demonstrate each element of style. But none is more crucial than force in fulfilling our responsibility to instruct, persuade, and move listeners to respond.[98] Consider four ways you can unleash force in your preaching.

Be Convicted

Several years ago I wrote a book entitled *The Passion Driven Sermon* (B & H, 2003). Shortly after it came out, a close friend called me and enthusiastically said, "I absolutely love your new book. What we need in preaching today is more passion!" I immediately knew he hadn't read the book. How? The book isn't about just being more passionate when we preach. It's about being passionate about the glory of God and then allowing that conviction to drive our preaching.

My friend was right, however. We do need more passion in preaching today. But we need passion that's inspired by the right stuff. Anybody can be passionate. I can turn on the TV late at night and watch some people on an infomercial passionately trying to sell me something I don't need. I've watched some politicians passionately appeal to their constituents about some principles I don't embrace. I've seen professional athletes passionately taunt their opponents. You can be passionate about the wrong stuff. But preachers are stewards of the right stuff, the best stuff in the world, the stuff that affects eternity. Of all people, we need to be passionate about what we preach, but our passion must be driven by our convictions about what is true.

There will always be a tight relationship between your theological convictions and how forceful you are in your preaching. Broadus says that energy in preaching closely relates to both subject matter and delivery. The preacher must believe in his subject and believe that what he says is important.[99] It's been said that force "demonstrates the conviction of the speaker and elicits conviction and decision from the hearer."[100] Your convictions about the person and work of Christ, the sovereignty of God, and other first-order doctrines in the Bible will contribute to a forceful delivery that impacts your listeners. The message of Christ's atoning death, bodily resurrection, and indwelling presence changes what the world calls ordinary men into world-changing preachers.

Your view of the Bible is particularly critical in affecting your force. The degree to which you are gripped by the inspiration, inerrancy, authority, and sufficiency of Scripture will have much to say about your presentation and whether or not people believe you. If your confidence in the Bible is shattered, you will have no sense of urgency to preach it. Unger says, "If the Bible is considered merely to contain the Word of God, rather than actually to be in toto the Word of God, there is naturally a decreased sense of responsibility to study its text minutely, or to systematize its theology, or authoritatively to declare its message."[101] A forceful preacher has to have a firm conviction that the Bible is God's Word. Such a persuasion will prove foundational in molding every part of your life, including your preaching.

Another important conviction that influences force is what you think about the call to preach, and particularly *your* call to preach. I'm concerned that fewer and fewer young men seem to be responding to God's call to preach and to pastor today. It's like everybody wants to do something else in Christianity but preach God's Word and pastor churches. I don't think God is calling fewer men to these tasks; I just think fewer are saying "yes" to His call.

Your conviction about your call to the preaching task will determine how you approach every preaching assignment. We have to preach with an awesome sense that God is preaching through us. That perspective is the only thing that will give you an appreciation and enthusiasm for delivering God's message. Chappell describes this wonder and the subsequent effect:

> [God] calls certain men to be his spokesmen because, knowing them, and knowing the world of which they are a part, he knows that they can do something for him that no one else can do. It is a thrilling and awe-inspiring thought that God has selected us for this high task in the knowledge that we can do this something that is essential to the salvation of men. In spite of all our handicaps, in spite of our limitations, if God has called us to preach, he has done so because he knows that we can do something for him that no one else can do.[102]

Fellow preacher, enter the pulpit believing you are doing something no one else can do in your particular situation. Sometimes that's the only thing that will keep you going. Sometimes in ministry leadership nothing else will get you up in the morning except your devotion to your preaching responsibilities.

Be Passionate

I love the story about David Hume and George Whitefield. Hume was a well-known Scottish philosopher and historian in the eighteenth century. And he was a deist. He didn't believe that the Bible was inspired or that Jesus was God's Son. But it's reported that he thought it was worthwhile to travel twenty miles to hear the evangelist George Whitefield preach. One morning, as he was headed down a street in London, he encountered a man who recognized him. The guy asked, "Aren't you David Hume?" "Yes," he replied. "Where are you going at this early hour?" the man asked. "I'm going to hear George Whitefield preach," Hume said. A bit puzzled, the man said, "You don't believe a word Whitefield preaches." "No," Hume answered, "but he does!"[103] Apparently George Whitefield *sounded* like he believed what he said!

Oh, I pray for that to be part of the commentary when people hear me preach—"He believes what he says!" While force in our preaching is rooted in our theological convictions, it needs to show up in the passion we demonstrate when we speak. Yes, we need to believe what we say, but we also need to say what we believe like we mean it and like we really want people to embrace it. We must preach passionately about what we passionately believe. No salesperson, politician, or athlete ought to out-passion preachers in the way they express what's important to them. Nothing is more important or relevant than the message of the Gospel!

Passion is the earnest and fervent drive born within the heart of the preacher. But it surfaces in a sincerity that provides us with the ability to make unusual appeal. While it emanates from our convictions about God's Word, it flows naturally in a pleasing rhythm when our hearts are engaged with a zeal to communicate it to our congregations.[104] The conviction of our hearts shows up in the communication of our lips. And not only does our passion for biblical truth affect the way we speak, it also creates a sense of wonder in our listeners. But your sermons won't hold any wonder for your listeners if they don't hold any wonder for you! When your convictions are manifested in your passion, they will adorn your sermons with wonder! And that wonder will influence your listeners to respond.

As you desire to make eternal truth known, earnestness will abound as your words are kindled by conviction and fanned by affection. Lewis challenges us:

> Dare to be intense. An earnest purpose gives intensity and urgency. . . . As sunlight can be focused to cut the hardest metals, as water can be concentrated to tear away the side of a mountain, as vapor can be compressed to move a locomotive, so the minister has persuasive power when he is genuinely earnest.[105]

This intensity, earnestness, and urgency regarding the Gospel message will be apparent to your people, and it will position them to decide rightly for the truth.

Sometimes your passion will be manifested through displays of emotion, and there's nothing wrong with that if those displays are sincere. A preacher's periodic emotional outbursts—prompted by sincere convictions about God's Word—can grab the attention of the audience and hold their interest captive. Genuine sadness, jubilation, anger, and other emotions should be unleashed and expressed in keeping with the content of the message. Jerry Vines and I are in agreement that modern preaching has become too dry-eyed. There needs to be a return to genuine, heartfelt weeping in the pulpit. Joel admonishes, "Between the vestibule and the altar let the priests, the ministers of the Lord, weep" (Joel 2: 17). Many preachers have lost their capacity to weep. They've become so professional, academic, and intellectual that they don't seem to feel what they say. There even seems to be an aversion to any expression of emotion in the pulpit. This affliction is not limited to liberal preachers. Many conservatives suffer from the same malady. Many of us are much too casual and matter-of-fact in our preaching.[106]

Our people would be helped to know that these are real men speaking to them, men who are broken for them and burdened for God's truth.

Weeping and other sincere expressions will sometimes result as we attempt to convince our listeners of the biblical message. Our burden for people to say "yes" to the truth can stir our hearts unexpectedly even as we're articulating our plea. But such expressions are not an end in and of themselves. What we want is for God to use our genuine emotion as a means of persuasion to action. Broadus notes that persuasive appeal is consistent with the practice of the prophets, Christ, and the apostles. They made impassioned appeals, not just to convince their hearers, but to incite them to action. Their language was filled with emotion.[107] Their passion produced a sense of urgency, an urgency born out of theological convictions and a passion for seeing their message change lives. May it be so with us.

Be Authoritative

When I was writing my dissertation on Richard Jackson's preaching, I remember running across some information about the impressions of people who heard him preach. While the growth of the North Phoenix Baptist Church during his tenure certainly is a testimony to the favorable attention of the masses, there were some who weren't as positive about his forceful style. A handful of people even accused him of being authoritarian and arrogant. I asked him about that perception in one of my interviews with him. I'll never forget what he said. He defended himself by saying that he went to the pulpit every time he preached believing he had heard from God. Consequently, he said, "I'm not asking a lot of questions; I'm giving a lot of answers."

I think there's a difference between being *authoritarian* and being *authoritative*. Some people get the two terms confused. And I fully realize that some people don't care about any difference and are turned off by both. But the distinction is incredibly important for preachers. To be *authoritarian* means to favor complete obedience or subjection as opposed to individual freedom. It's often used for governments, dictators, and political systems who exercise complete control over the will of others. To be *authoritative*, on the other hand, means to have due authority, or the sanction or weight of authority, and that usually supported by documentary evidence. As preachers, we must never give the air of being *authoritarian* when we preach, but we must always be *authoritative* with what we preach. After all, our authority is supported by documentary evidence—God's written Word!

I listened to Jackson preach a lot. I think his critics confused *authoritarian* and *authoritative*. Or maybe they didn't care. Maybe they just didn't like somebody who was just giving a lot of answers without asking a lot of questions. But what's for sure is that he had an *authoritative* tone when he spoke, and that tone flowed from his certainty about two things—his message and his role as the messenger. His force grew out of his conviction about the message of the biblical text he was preaching. He believed he was speaking on behalf of God. And that's what every preacher of the Gospel should do every time he stands to preach.

The people who listened to Jesus didn't conclude that He was speaking as an authoritarian. But they did hear Him as one who had authority, distinguishing His message and demeanor from that of the scribes they were accustomed to hearing. When He finished teaching in the synagogue in Capernaum, the people "were astonished at his teaching, for he taught them as one who had authority, and not as the scribes" (Mark 1:22). Basically, they were saying, "That guy's not from around here." They had never heard anybody speak like He spoke. I think that was the same conclusion at which those disciples on the road to Emmaus arrived. After Jesus left their presence, they rhetorically asked, "Did not our hearts burn within us while he talked to us on the road, while he opened to us the Scriptures?" (Luke 24:32). Something gave them the impression they had just heard from a guy who was from a different planet!

The apostle Paul believed that he preached with an authority from heaven. Notice his emphasis on the stewardship of his calling in 2 Corinthians:

> All this is from God, who through Christ reconciled us to himself and *gave us the ministry of reconciliation*; that is, in Christ God was reconciling the world to himself, not counting their trespasses against them, and *entrusting to us the message of reconciliation*. Therefore, *we are ambassadors for Christ, God making his appeal through us*. We

> implore you on behalf of Christ, be reconciled to God. (2 Cor. 5:18-20; emphasis mine)

He knew he had been commissioned by God to speak on His behalf, and that his faithfulness to that task was people's only hope of reconciliation. To the Colossians he wrote: "I became a minister according to the stewardship from God that was given to me for you, to make the word of God fully known" (Col 1:25). Paul preached authoritatively because God had charged him to do so. Furthermore, God had ordained Paul's authoritative proclamation to be Plan A for reconciling people to Himself. Preacher, that's still His Plan A, and He has no Plan B.

Authoritative speech exudes force in the preaching event and, subsequently, fosters spiritual decisions. When we preach—not on our own authority but on the authority of God's Word—something other-worldly happens. People hear God's voice and not ours. As a result, they put their faith not in the wisdom of a man but in the power of God (cf. 1 Cor. 2:5). Brothers, we should pray to this end whenever we preach. We should ask God to give us grace to speak authoritatively in His stead and to cause His Word to burn within the hearts of the people who hear us.

People who listen to sermons aren't the only ones who sometimes confuse being authoritative with being authoritarian. Some preachers do it as well. Consequently, they sacrifice their preaching authority for a false sense of humility, which is really nothing more than debilitating doubt. Achtemeier warns:

> Let us never mistake doubt in the pulpit for humility. Sometimes preachers are so worried about taking notice of every point of view and so fearful of imposing their own thoughts on their people, that they preach a Gospel

> framed in the terms of "it may be." . . . We know whom we have believed, and there is no doubt about his victory. Only if our style conveys that certainty can our people have any hope at all.[108]

People want and need us to speak God's Word to them. It's their only hope of real life change.

While there are many ways we can express force in our preaching, let me offer one easy practice that carries a big stick. Use imperative language. Don't shy away from telling people straight up to do something God's Word tells them to do. I know that many preachers and teachers of preaching are saying the opposite today, but I think it's with little foundation. Jesus and His apostles used a lot of imperative language, and so should we. Use words and phrases that explicitly call for action or response. Speak with language that clearly demands that listeners either embrace a truth or act on it.

The use of imperative language is totally consistent with the general objective of persuasion. We've already established that the intent of the sermon naturally is related to the call for action. Broadus says the sermon objective is concerned with actions, changes, and verdict by answering the question, "What life changes should result from the sermon?"[109] Donald Miller contends, "The aim consists in what we desire that truth [the theme of the sermon] to do to the hearer, or what we desire the hearer to do in response to the truth."[110] So why should we be hesitant about telling people what they ought to do? Preacher, utilize language that calls on listeners to dedicate all their time, talent, and personality to God. Don't be afraid to charge them to do so.

Be Free

Let me put my cards on the table. I wish every preacher preached without notes. But I don't believe the degree of notes a guy uses in his preaching is a spiritual thing. While I personally don't use notes when I preach, I have very close friends who use full manuscripts, and they follow them pretty much word-for-word. And many people would testify that some of those guys preach with more power and greater effectualness than I do. I won't argue with that. I believe some guys have an intellectual capacity that enables them to navigate a manuscript in preaching that most of the rest of us don't. They can use a lot of notes without it being apparent. But the average preacher can't do that. When most of us use a lot of notes, it looks like we're using them heavily, if not reading them closely. And that will always influence the degree to which we engage our listeners, as well as the force that moves them to decision.

Decisional force, however, is not technically an issue of whether or not we use notes when we preach. It's not so much about the degree of notes we use, but how we navigate our notes, and how that navigation affects our engagement with the audience. Some preachers follow full manuscripts when they preach. Others don't use any notes. And there are guys who use everything in between. The issue is whether or not we're able to freely engage the listeners so every one of them believes we're talking to them. Let's be honest. When we listen to a sermon, we can tell when we feel like the preacher is talking to us. But we can also tell when it feels like he is up there talking and we just happen to be in the room. There's a huge difference between the two. I think it's the difference between really preaching and just delivering a sermon.

Regardless of the degree of notes you use, the force of decisional impact will be heightened by the way you deliver your sermons.

Most—if not all—of the preachers in the Bible obviously preached without notes, yet they preached powerfully and prompted lots of decision for the Gospel. It's hard to imagine Jesus on the site of the Sermon on the Mount or Peter at Pentecost unfolding a piece of parchment on which they'd scribbled their sermon notes. Many of the great expositors throughout the history of the church have preached the same way and seen similar results. Alexander Maclaren prepared his sermons very carefully, more carefully than if he were planning to read them or recite them from memory. He would allow the words to well up in his heart and then unleash them at the moment of delivery. G. Campbell Morgan, that "Prince of Expositors," did the same. Morgan believed that using a manuscript or notes interfered with the eye contact characteristic of animated conversation.[111]

That's why I challenge preachers to consider preaching without notes as the default. Start there and work hard to develop the skill. Write out a full manuscript as part of your preparation, prayerfully internalize your content and flow of thought through in-depth review. But then get up and preach it without any notes. Brown, Clinard, and Northcutt highlight the benefit of this approach:

> It has every advantage of other delivery options without their inherent disadvantages. Like the manuscript [reading] and memory methods, it affords the most careful preparation, but it does not limit audience rapport or pulpit freedom. Like the extemporaneous method, it demands creative thought during delivery and affords maximum rhetorical excellence while at the same time demanding more rigorous preparation.[112]

This approach certainly can be modified by taking a manuscript or some other degree of notes into the pulpit, but only referring to them selectively. But experiment with no notes first. If your delivery absolutely continues to crash and burn after sincere efforts, then experiment with using varying degrees of notes. But start off assuming you'll preach with the freedom of not being tied to anything but your Bible and any markings you might make in its margins.

While I believe God's Spirit is working in our preparation long before we actually preach, I do think there's something mysterious that happens in the preaching moment. The Spirit is at work in a unique way. Learning to deliver your sermon freely will bring a great sense of freshness in your expression. When you reserve at least some of your expression for the moment of delivery, you make room for all the variable factors involved in effective speech. Broadus describes this dynamic involved in thorough preparation and free delivery:

> If, full of his theme and impressed with its importance, he [the preacher] presently secures the interested and sympathizing attention of even a few good listeners, and the fire of his eyes comes reflected back from theirs, . . . he cannot fail sometimes to strike out thoughts more splendid and more precious than ever visit his mind in solitary musing.[113]

Free delivery maximizes the best of both worlds. It's a powerful medium of *informed* spontaneous expression, allowing for the fruit of your study to be expressed in the most natural and forceful way.

Listeners are more likely to retain a much higher percentage of a sermon's content when it's delivered freely. Audience reactions are more sympathetic and more attentive when preachers speak *to* their listeners and not just *over* them. Robinson observes that relying heavily on notes in the preaching event detracts from sermon force. He says that

> a sermon is not an essay on its hind legs. Since what [the preacher] writes serves only as a broad preparation for what he will actually say, the manuscript is not a preacher's final product. A sermon should not be read to a congregation. Reading kills the lively sense of communication.[114]

The message will be less forceful when it's read because it appears to be wooden and presented without conviction.

Again, the issue here isn't the degree of notes. It's how you use your notes. It's whether or not you're able to look your listeners in the eye and speak directly to them. If you do use a manuscript or another degree of notes, work hard to avoid the pitfalls of reading from those notes. Make sure you get your message in your heart and not just in your head. Become so familiar with your notes during the preparation process that any dependence upon them during delivery is all but eliminated. Being able to memorize portions of your content can be advantageous. Robinson says, "The minister who memorizes easily and speaks naturally from memory can attain heights of rhetorical excellence in the pulpit which are enviable."[115] But be careful with memorizing your whole sermon. A memorized manuscript usually sounds like it's memorized, and it comes across much like reading it.

When you preach freely, you preach conversationally. Conversational speech doesn't mean pulling up a stool and having a fireside chat. It means speaking naturally, like we do in normal conversation. In normal conversation we use inflection, we adjust our volume and rate, and we look whoever we're talking to in the eyes. Conversational speech is forceful because it's natural and animated. Blackwood says:

> This means enthusiasm in talking things over with the hearers. It means using all the charm, the variety, and the winsomeness that mark spirited talk at its best. Here stands no dictator sending down pontifical deliverances from some Olympian height, no advocate at the bar defending the Bible as though it were about to be executed. Here speaks a friend, opening up a truth that he has discovered in the Book, and meeting a need that he has found among the people.[116]

You will capitalize on the decisional benefit of natural, animated speech when you preach freely. You will apply and argue your message genuinely from your heart.

Free delivery largely is a matter of the mental attitude of the preacher. Relevant information is underscored by his natural physical presentation of the sermon. Extemporaneous application and argumentation grows out of an inner motivation in his soul. We all want to communicate the relevance of our message to our listeners. This impulse is best manifested in natural body action that can't be planned. Our movements should be based on convictions about which we feel deeply, and we want our listeners to feel deeply about them as well. The best way for this to happen is for us to let those convictions be expressed naturally.

SUMMARY

Tying it all together, lack of sermon force often is interpreted as lack of conviction. Lack of conviction—or even just the perception of it—betrays a lack of passion. When conviction and passion are absent, the preacher never comes across as having any real spiritual authority. This void undermines real freedom in the pulpit. When the preacher has no freedom and no sermon force, listeners are abandoned to a cloud of indecision.

Conversely, the man who is full of biblical conviction will be driven by supernatural passion that endues him with real spiritual authority and freedom in the pulpit. Listeners will be engaged by a man they perceive has come from God to speak to them on His behalf. They will be gripped by the interweaving of truth and power through the spiritual force of the sermon. When this scenario exists, listeners are led to the inevitable point of decision. God has spoken. They have heard. Transformation has been ushered to the doorstep of their hearts, awaiting only their agreement with God's truth.

Brothers, let's be preachers whose sermon force is palpable, whose conviction and passion are Spirit given, whose authority and freedom are Spirit driven, and whose audiences decide for real biblical living.

CHAPTER VI

PUBLIC EXPRESSIONS OF SPIRITUAL DECISIONS

"Hi, my name is Jim, and I believe in giving expression to spiritual decisions regarding the preached Word." There, I've said it. I think there can be value in giving people the opportunity to give expression to their spiritual responses to God's Word, and to even do so publicly and immediately upon hearing and receiving it. While I don't believe such expressions are required for authentic spiritual decision-making, I do think they can help with the process in healthy, spiritual ways. They can drive a stake in a spiritual decision, connect a struggling listener with someone who can give them counsel, provide helpful confirmation to a response, and even affirm and encourage the faith community.

This particular issue is likely another area in which many of us have thrown the baby out with the bathwater in our reaction to gross abuses. So, as we bring this conversation on decisional preaching to a close, let me offer some of my thoughts on this tenuous subject.

My goal here is not to offer a biblical defense or theological rationale for extending calls for people to express their spiritual decisions. I've made attempts at that before, standing on the shoulders of others who did it even better before me.[117] Here, I prayerfully just want to be pastoral, practical, and helpful. Consider three challenges when it comes to calling for expressions of response.

TAKE THE RISK

I'll never forget that winter night in January of 1983. My wife and I stood at a church altar in El Paso, Texas, and said "I do" to one another. We entered into a covenant in which we agreed to be one another's partner for the rest of our time on earth. We made verbal commitments to one another "to have and to hold, from this day forward, for better, for worse, for richer, for poorer, in sickness and in health, to love and to cherish, till death do us part." And as a public expression of the vows we were making, we not only made them in front of a crowd of witnesses, but we exchanged rings that we've worn on our fingers for over thirty-five years now. We signed up for life, and we wanted everybody to know it!

My wife and I understand that the ceremony we had doesn't constitute our marriage. Our marriage is the covenant love we've shared for almost four decades. Because a marriage is hard work, we've had to renew our vows every day in order to make our relationship survive and thrive. That doesn't happen just because you stand at an altar and say you're committed to making it work in front of some witnesses. But at the same time, our ceremony—including the vows and the rings and the witnesses—upped the ante several notches when it came to our commitment. We not only vocalized our resolve to one another; we did it in front of a bunch of people who can testify that we did it. And we've worn rings on our fingers ever since so everybody knows we did it! Our personal covenant has been served well by our public ceremony.

The public wedding ceremony isn't without risks, ones that potentially can lead to false commitments and broken marriages. For example, it's possible that a couple will equate their ceremony with the covenant into which they're entering, as opposed to seeing it merely as an initial public expression of their commitments that have to be renewed every day. Or they may see their vows as reflecting a relationship that's the result of their initiative as opposed to one "God has joined together" (Matt 19:6). It's even possible that the public nature of such an emotional and tender event could innocently motivate an unmarried person attending the wedding to hurry out afterwards and get married themselves, and to do so prematurely.

One of the biggest risks in a wedding ceremony is the one pastors run by putting words in the mouths of couples. Most often we ask them to repeat their vows after us. A bride and groom can easily see the reciting of their vows as nothing more than repeating words for the sake of tradition as opposed to the articulation of sincere and heart-felt resolve. Similarly, the idea of leading someone in a "sinner's prayer" for salvation gets a lot of flak because of this very risk. It is kind of curious to me that many preachers who vehemently criticize the idea of leading someone to repeat a prayer for salvation have no problem standing at an altar and asking a couple to repeat the vows of covenant marriage. Both salvation and covenant marriage are weighty matters that demand our careful handling.

None of these risks, however, keep us from encouraging and enjoying the blessings and benefits of a wedding ceremony. Why? Because we understand the sanctity of the covenant and the value of a public expression that represents it. We know that the ceremony isn't the essence of a couple's love for one another or even of their commitment to spend their lives together. We also know, however, that it can be a meaningful start to their life-long journey with each other. While we're very conscious that the Bible doesn't mandate people to stand at church altars in front of witnesses or exchange rings as an expression of wedding vows, we know that doing so can provide a meaningful and memorializing beginning to a covenant relationship.

Because we understand the value and are willing to take some risks, the church trusts pastors and other ministry leaders to shepherd couples and lead congregations to approach wedding ceremonies rightly. I think the same thing can be done with giving people the opportunity to give public expression to spiritual decisions. If we take the risk of training pastors and other ministry leaders to shepherd people well who are deciding for Gospel truth, we can capitalize on the rewards that come with it. Great value can be attained when people are offered the opportunity to give expression to spiritual decisions they're making in response to the preached Word. We can attain that value if we will shepherd people to do it with integrity. We won't attain it if we just avoid it altogether because of the risk.

Let's be clear—baptism is the only biblically mandated public profession of faith and, therefore, the only one the church should require. Baptism's value, however, certainly can be replicated when preacher's give listeners the chance to physically express their spiritual decisions in response to a sermon from God's Word. Physical expressions can add accountability to a decision, memorialize a spiritual marker, heighten memory of a commitment, or help to drive a stake in a person's resolve. All of these benefits and more can serve to foster faithfulness in living out the decision being made. Therein, they add both psychological and spiritual value to the response to God's Word.

If we're honest, we know that the same risks mentioned above regarding the wedding ceremony are true for many acts of corporate worship in which we ask people to participate regularly. We often expect everyone to stand and sing praises, but we never give a second thought to the risk of some attenders doing so insincerely, feeling pressured to participate simply because everyone else is doing it. In many churches offering plates are passed without the slightest concern that someone might be manipulated to give simply because the person next to them is giving or that they may give in order to gain indulgence from God. In most of our worship gatherings we at some point invite the congregation to bow their heads and pray, but we're never concerned that some participants may go through the motions and never mean it but only do it because everyone else is doing it.

All of these practices and more could be considered mockeries of worship and acts that lead people to a false sense of relationship with God. We're willing to run the risks, however, because we believe that with good leadership we can shepherd people through these risky waters and attain a higher and more noble reward. We're willing to navigate the sometimes-muddy waters of certain worship forms because we think there's great value in the body of Christ experiencing their function. The same is true for offering the opportunity for people to give expression to what's going on in their hearts, and to sometimes even invite them to do it publicly and immediately upon hearing God's Word. While it's not a mandate from the Bible, it can be meaningful for the individual worshiper and the congregation...*if* preachers are willing to take the risk.

USE A VARIETY OF MODELS

My mom is closing in on eighty years old, and she loves Jesus. She rarely misses her personal worship time in the early morning hours of each day. Her prayer life puts mine to shame. She faithfully serves in her local church, and she does some mentoring and disciple-making through a bi-monthly sewing group she hosts in her home. She shares her faith regularly. My mom clearly demonstrates her faith in Christ and gives evidence of being one of His disciples. But if you declared that the test of sincere faith and authentic fellowship in Christ was getting on an elevator, going up to the top of a fifty-story building, and standing up on the ledge, my sweet little 4'11" godly mom probably isn't playing. Why? Because she's acrophobic. She loves Jesus, but—like her son—she's afraid of heights!

One of the mistakes pastors have made in calling for expressions of response as part of their preaching is using the same model every time and employing that model as the litmus test for sincerity of heart. As I mentioned before, the traditional altar call for people to come to the front of the auditorium has been the most prevalent model used in many circles, including my own denomination. I'm convinced that the regularity and exclusivity of this approach, however, is one thing that's not only caused it to lose meaning for many congregations but also has caused some preachers to react against it and some sincere worshipers never to respond to it.

Doing any worship element—including preaching—the exact same way over and over again runs the risk of lessening its value and causing it to become dead weight for worshipers, especially if worship leaders don't navigate it well. Some people can easily begin to presume upon it and see it as routine. Others may be made to feel inadequate because it exposes a natural phobia, not a disingenuous heart. So, if you decide to include a call for expressions of response to all or some of your messages, let me encourage you to use a variety of models. But be aware that any model you use will have both advantages and disadvantages, so you need to be creative, intentional, and meaningful as you apply each one. And you need to apply them with integrity, because whatever expression of response you invite people to give, you're asking them to give it in response to the Gospel. And that means we're bound to the highest degree of integrity mankind can attain. Here are some models to consider.[118]

Vocal expression. Probably the most common expression of response used in most public worship events are various kinds of verbal replies offered by participants. Certainly, the most familiar vocal expression of response in Scripture—and in contemporary culture—is people singing as part of corporate worship (e.g., Exod 15:1; Pss 147:1; 149:1; Col 3:16; cf. Eph 5:19). You might consider periodically following the preaching event by inviting the congregation to sing a song or songs in direct response to what you just preached. In addition to singing, people may respond with expressions of agreement like "Amen." At other times they may shout to the Lord (e.g., Lev 9:24; 1 Sam 4:5; 2 Sam 6:15; 1 Chron 15:28; Ezra 3:11; Ps. 27:6; Matt 21:9). These vocalized responses to God's Word may be spontaneous (e.g., Neh 8:6) or prompted by worship leaders (e.g., Pss 33:1; 47:1), but they should always be navigated with integrity.

Physical gesture. Another simple way of giving people an opportunity to express their response is to ask for some type of physical gesture in response to the message. People may be asked to stand, bow, kneel, or raise their hands as an indication of their heart's decision. Again, we have numerous biblical examples of these kinds of responses (e.g., Neh 8:6; Ps 134:2; 1 Tim 2:8). Sometimes such expressions are spontaneous;

other times they are prompted by a worship leader. People may be invited to offer a particular gesture while the rest of the congregation is praying with their eyes closed. I've asked people to stand as an expression of commitment in response to a message from Daniel 3 about not following the cultural crowd in worshiping idols. I've invited people to kneel by their seats as an indication of resolve to give themselves to new heights in prayer. I've even asked people to stand while everyone else was watching as a testimony of confessing Christ after an evangelistic message. Regardless of the specific gesture that's requested, it should always be purposeful and in keeping with the idea in the text.

Written record. A semi-public expression of response that's popular today is to ask people to indicate their decision on a card or some other form. This invitation offers the opportunity to express a response immediately, but more privately. Good decision cards usually list a number of possible spiritual responses but also include a place for people to write in their own words what they're feeling, sensing, or desiring in response to the preached Word. You might use a card when asking for people to confess specific sins that don't need to be publicized to everyone. You may use one when lots of people are present who aren't familiar with the whole idea of public responses. Or you might invite people to record questions or just indicate a desire to talk to someone about their spiritual journey. One logistical issue that should always be addressed when using this model is determining in advance a prudent and judicious means of collecting the decision cards. Preachers need to give simple and clear instructions regarding what responders are to do with their cards.

Physical relocation. The most familiar expression of response in many traditions, including my own, is what I would call the physical relocation model. It's variously called the "invitation" or the "altar call." It involves inviting responders to physically relocate from their seats, moving to another place in or near the worship room in response to the preached Word. The advantage of this model is that it gives responders the opportunity for immediate and physical response. Its public nature drives a psychological stake in the responders' spiritual decisions while providing the opportunity to get additional guidance. Like some of the gesture examples I gave above, be sure to match whatever you ask people to do with your preaching text and its primary audience. Certainly, asking them to come to the front of the worship room may be conducive for many messages. But in response to a message on reconciling with other believers, maybe inviting responders to go to fellow church members in the audience with whom they have grievances is a better fit. Or you might ask people to go to a designated counseling area or inquiry room other than the front of the worship area.

Post-meeting ministry. An invitation model that's not as immediate and not as public involves inviting people to respond by attending some kind of ministry session after the worship event is over. This model is a contemporary form of the old inquiry room used by many preachers in the nineteenth and early twentieth centuries. The idea is to invite responders to a private or semiprivate meeting with the preacher or other trained leader either immediately after the service or at some time in the near future so they can ask questions, receive further counsel, or offer some extended expression of a commitment. In response to a sermon from Luke 9:57–62, for example, the preacher might invite responders to attend a meeting one night the following week to ask questions and get more information on true discipleship. After preaching from Psalm 101:3 on guarding our eyes, you may challenge people to go home, collect in a paper sack any seductive printed or recorded materials, and return at a prescribed time to a designated location to join others in discarding the items in a meaningful way.

Multiple approach. One of my favorite ways to call for expressions of response to the preached Word is to offer more than one way for people to act within the same invitation. The opportunity for multiple ways for people to respond is more conducive for the variety of levels of spiritual maturity and possible spiritual decisions that characterize any given congregation at any given time in any size of church. A three-tiered invitation, for example, might involve a traditional altar call, followed by the use of a decision card provided for those who don't feel comfortable with going to the altar, followed by a third call for still others to meet with available encouragers at a designated place after the worship gathering. If at all possible, avoid using only one particular expression of response (like the altar call) and making it the determinant of sincerity. Some people—like my mom who I mentioned earlier—struggle with natural phobias that might hinder them from responding in one particular way. Providing multiple ways for people to respond opens other doors for more people at various places in the spiritual journey to express their decisions.

APPEAL WITH INTEGRITY

We need to make sure that when we call for expressions of response that we do so in the most appropriate ways. By appropriate, I mean appropriate first to the integrity of the Gospel, second to our immediate preaching texts, and third to the hearers we're inviting to respond. While there are many suggestions we could discuss at this point, let me offer five particularly important qualities of healthy calls for people to give expression to their spiritual responses.[119]

Don't manipulate. Let's start with this basic issue of integrity. Jesus tells us that as long as the church is on earth, it will be plagued by false decisions and unregenerate members (see Matt 7:15-23; 13:1-30). This reality makes it imperative that preachers don't manipulate people to make spiritual decisions. When you're appealing to people to decide rightly for Gospel truth, never coerce them, pressure them, play on their emotions, or make them feel guilty about not rising above their natural fears. Every call for response—especially one that's public in nature—should be handled in such a way that when a person responds to the preacher's appeal, he or she isn't devastated by unexpectedly being put up in front of a crowd without proper preparation. In addition to calls that are threatening to certain temperaments, avoid bait-and-switch techniques, intentional embarrassment, misleading directions, wrongfully playing on people's emotions, trying to set the mood with certain lighting and music, or prolonged appeals that wear people down physically.

Make it cohesive. Cohesiveness between the message and the call for expressions of response influences decision-making because it helps the sermon to flow smoothly. The absence of cohesiveness, on the other hand, will likely distract the listeners. Here are some ways to make your call cohesive with the rest of your message. First, as I've already said, match your call for response with your message. Don't immediately follow a message on the Christian life with a call for persons to receive Christ, and vice versa. Your call for response should flow directly from your sermon and the primary audience of the biblical text. Second, don't always reserve your call for response for the end of your sermon. It can be helpful to build toward the call for response from the very beginning by telling people early in your sermon what you're going to ask them to do in response to the message. Third, approach your sermon conclusion as a transition to—or even synonymous with—your call for response. This will prevent the call for response from appearing to be an addendum to your message or a completely separate part of the worship event. Fourth, include sincere appeal and persuasion as a major part of your sermon conclusion. Don't call people to weighty, eternal spiritual decisions in a lifeless way as if you're some clerical version of a wimpy cartoon character. Fifth, include exhortation to some specific application as part of your call for response. Plead with people to say "yes" to the truth you're preaching. Sixth, make a smooth transition into your call for response. Sloppy transitions and abrupt breaks can distract potential responders.

Be simple and clear. Decisional impact will increase in relation to the audience's understanding about the expected response. Consequently, calls for expressions of response have to be extremely simple and clear. A preacher's failure to provide clear and specific instructions can cheapen the appeal and adversely affect genuine decisions, not to mention compromising the luster and glory of the Gospel. Articulate the Gospel clearly and provide listeners clear instructions about how to be saved. Be equally clear when you're calling on believers to express their decisions. Make clear distinction between the response you're expecting from believers and those you're expecting from unbelievers. Whatever you do, avoid giving the impression that walking an aisle is synonymous with regeneration. People may be saved while you're preaching, or after responding physically and getting connected to someone for counsel, or even while walking an aisle or raising their hand or standing up in response to your invitation. But that's not your business. You're responsible for explaining the Gospel clearly and accurately, calling people to decide for it, and then following up with them to confirm their understanding and provide further ministry. So, clearly distinguish the call for repentance, faith, and public discipleship from the physical expression of public response. For both believers and unbelievers, tell them exactly and specifically what they're being asked to do, why they're being asked to do it, and what will take place when they do it. And avoid intricacy and elaboration when it comes to giving instructions. Get directly to the point, avoid verbosity and ornate terms and overly religious or liturgical language. Whatever you do, don't try to be profound, professional, and polished. Just be clear, simple, and concise.

Have a good plan. One of the most neglected parts of extending effective calls for expressions of response is planning ahead. Many preachers and other church leaders never think through the logistics of how they're going to call people to express their decisions or what's going to happen when they do. When people respond, you need to have a good plan in place that will enable you and your faith family to come alongside them in their spiritual journey. Train some of your leaders to be available to offer encouragement and other ministry to people who are making spiritual decisions. Make sure you have more than one person to receive people when they respond. Otherwise, no one else is likely to respond if there's no one available for them. And be sure to investigate all legal issues that relate to people offering counsel in situations like this, and then train your people accordingly.

Present the Gospel every time. Even when your message has been primarily directed at believers, be sure to turn every appeal at some strategic point to the invitation for salvation. Again, always extend your first call for response to the primary intended audience of your preaching text. If your passage primarily is speaking to believers, invite them first to act upon the given truth. But before you shut your response time down and dismiss the congregation or move on to other worship elements, make sure you appeal to unbelievers to repent of sin and trust in Christ. At the same time, don't feel like you have to wait until the end of the sermon to make this appeal. Even if your preaching text is primarily aimed at believers, look for various points in the message that you can directly address unbelievers and share the Gospel with them.

Have at least one synopsis—or capsule—of the Gospel that you can use in every message (e.g., 1 Cor 15:3–4; 2 Tim 1:8–10). For me, I rarely preach a sermon that at some point I don't say something like:

> Jesus came to earth and lived a life that you can't live, meeting God's standard of perfection for getting into heaven. Then He took that perfect life to the cross and died a death you should've died, incurring God's wrath against your sin on your behalf. Then He defeated death and the grave by rising again, buying the right to give you back the life God created you to have. And He'll give it to you right now if you'll change your mind about your sin and trust Him alone to save you.[120]

While this Gospel capsule isn't perfect, it's at least one stab at including a summary of the whole Gospel in every sermon. You will do well to have several of these kinds of Gospel digests in your preaching pocket. So look for strategic places in sermons to deposit your Gospel capsules. But whatever you do, make sure that before the sermon is over, you clearly bottom-line the whole Gospel at least once and appeal for unbelievers to embrace it.[121]

SUMMARY

I hate throwing the baby out with the bathwater. We're so inclined to do that. We see an abuse of something, and we react against it. But we not only react against it, we react to the other extreme. I've seen people in my own church tradition react to abuses in charismatic worship and then render as taboo some very biblical expressions like raising and clapping hands. I've seen preachers react to cheesy alliteration and end up blackballing an approach that can be very helpful to listeners when used with integrity. Throwing the baby out with the bathwater is part of our nature. I'm just making one simple appeal here: Let's don't do that when it comes to calling for physical expressions of spiritual decisions regarding the preached Word. Yes, it's been abused. But let's fix it instead of killing it. You don't have to call for physical expressions, but it can be a meaningful tool to have in your toolbox. Even if you don't use it, don't hate on others that do so as long as they're doing it well.

CONCLUSION

"WE PERSUADE MEN"

Another one of my favorite professors at Southwestern Seminary was Dr. Curtis Vaughan. He taught New Testament and Greek. Some of my favorite classes were his "Preaching from" courses. I took him for "Preaching from Galatians" and "Preaching from Colossians" and several other elective courses. I remember one day listening to him talk about election. He said one of the criticisms he had heard about election was that it dulled the blade of evangelism. "Actually," he said, "the doctrine of election sharpens the blade of evangelism for me because it tells me there will always be some people out there who say 'yes'!"

Regardless of what you believe about election, the Gospel "is the power of God to salvation to everyone who believes" (Rom 1:16). And because of that innate quality, we can be confident there will always be some people who will say "yes" to it. That should be enough to compel us to call on people—both believers and unbelievers—to decide for it. So, this little book has a big ask. I'm asking you today to resolve to preach decisionally—to invite, to call, to beg, to plead, to appeal, to persuade, to exhort. I'm inviting you today to decide to be a decisional preacher.

Maybe you would be so compelled to press pause for a moment before reading on, bow your head and heart, and tell our Lord of your resolve.

The Apostle Paul said, "Knowing the fear of the Lord, we persuade others. But what we are is known to God" (2 Co. 5:11). The verb translated "persuade" indicates that Paul persuaded others by God's means and according to God's standards, not with the trappings of adorned rhetoric, seductive manipulation, or heavy-handed authority. Instead, "he trusts in the merits of the Gospel, paradoxical and scandalous as it is, to pass any honest scrutiny and allows his hearers to decide for themselves its truth."[122] And so must we.

Maybe the most compelling reason we have for decisional preaching is found when Paul's words in 2 Corinthians 5:11 are connected with his claim a little bit later in the chapter. He writes,

> All this is from God, who through Christ reconciled us to himself and gave us the ministry of reconciliation; that is, in Christ God was reconciling the world to himself, not counting their trespasses against them, and entrusting to us the message of reconciliation. Therefore, we are ambassadors for Christ, God making his appeal through us. We implore you on behalf of Christ, be reconciled to God. (2 Cor 5:18–20)

I'm struck by the stewardship implied in the fact that He "gave us the ministry of reconciliation" and is "entrusting to us the message of reconciliation." The ministry and the message—What a trust!

While the deposits of the ministry and the message of reconciliation overwhelm me, I'm haunted by something else in the text: "God making his appeal through us." Ah, this is what puts Paul's assertion in 5:11 in proper context. Yes, we persuade others as ones charged with both the ministry and the message of reconciliation. We persuade people in the fear of the Lord, the One to whom "what we are is known," the One who knows our every motive, and yet the One who is "making his appeal through us." By God's divine ordination, we are commissioned to persuade people on His behalf, as His mouthpieces! And we do it in a straightforward and honorable way as ones who must answer to Him.

Brothers, this is God's Plan A, and He has no Plan B. Let's persuade people for the Gospel with integrity, and let's appeal to them to decide rightly for it. Let's persuade men, women, boys and girls—not with polished oratory and secular sales strategies—but with the glorious Gospel of Christ, trusting it to do its work through us. Let's appeal to them with a broken heart and an urgent tone, praying they will decide rightly for it. There will always be some out there who will say "yes" with genuine hearts.

ENDNOTES

1. Roy Fish, *How to Give an Evangelistic Invitation*, produced by the Baptist General Convention of Texas, 44 min., Dallas, TX, 1991, videocassette.
2. Charles S. Kelley, Jr., *Fuel the Fire: Lessons from the History of Southern Baptist Evengelism* (B&H, 2018), 60.
3. Ibid., 57.
4. Ibid., 53.
5. Jason Allen, "On Preaching and Public Invitations," *For the Church*, https://ftc.co/resource-library/blog-entries/on-preaching-and-public-invitations, accessed March 5, 2018
6. See V. L. Stanfield, *Effective Evangelistic Preaching* (Grand Rapids: Baker Book House, 1965), 22-24.
7. Richard A. Jackson, "When a Man Comes Close, Part 2," sermon preached at the North Phoenix Baptist Church based on Acts 26:1-32, 20 November 1983, manuscript, 24-25.
8. Charles H. Spurgeon, *The New Park Street Pulpit*, Vol. V (Pasadena, Texas: Pilgrim Publications, 1981), 120.
9. Charles H. Spurgeon, *The Metropolitan Tabernacle Pulpit*, Vol. XV (Pasadena, Texas: Pilgrim Publications, 1984), 458.
10. Charles H. Spurgeon, *The Metropolitan Tabernacle Pulpit*, Vol. LVI (Pasadena, Texas: Pilgrim Publications, 1979), 631.
11. Steven J. Lawson, *The Gospel Focus of Charles Spurgeon* A Long Line

of Godly Men 4 (Sanford, FL: Reformation Trust, 2012), 62.
12. Jason Allen, "On Preaching and Public Invitations," Forhttps://ftc.co/resource-library/blog-entries/on-preaching-and-public-invitations, accessed March 5, 2018.
13. Edwin Charles Dargan, A History of Preaching, vol. 1 (New York: Burt Franklin, 1905; reprint, New York: Burt Franklin, 1968), 14 (page reference is to reprint edition).
14. Lester Thonssen, ed., Selected Readings in Rhetoric and Public Speaking (New York: Wilson Press, 1942), 36.
15. Thomas D. Lea and Hayne P. Griffin, Jr., 1, 2 Timothy, Titus, New American Commentary 34 (Nashville: Broadman & Holman, 1992), 138.
16. John F. MacArthur, Jr., 1 Timothy (Chicago: Moody, 1995), 176.
17. Ralph Earle, 1 Timothy. The Expositor's Bible Commentary, vol. 11: Ephesians through Philemon, ed. F. E. Gaebelein (Grand Rapids: Zondervan, 1981), 374.
18. George W. Knight, III, The Pastoral Epistles: A Commentary on the Greek Text (Grand Rapids: Eerdmans, 1992), 207–8.
19. C. H. Spurgeon, "Saving Great Sinners with a Great Salvation," in Great Preaching on Salvation, comp. Curtis Hutson (Murfreesboro, TN: Sword of the Lord, 1993), 198.
20. C. H. Spurgeon, "The Silver Trumpet," A Sermon Delivered on March 24, 1861, at Exeter Hall, Strand, https://answersingenesis.org/education/spurgeon-sermons/366-the-silver-trumpet, accessed March 12, 2018.
21. C. H. Spurgeon, "How to Win Souls for Christ," in How to Promote and Conduct a Successful Revival (Chicago: Fleming H. Revell, 1901), 216.
22. J. Daniel Baumann, An Introduction to Contemporary Preaching (Grand Rapids: Baker, 1972), 205.
23. John MacArthur, Jr., "Frequently Asked Questions About Expository Preaching," in Rediscovering Expository Preaching, ed. Richard L.

Mayhue (Dallas: Word, 1992), 343.
24. Allen, "On Preaching and Public Invitations."
25. Derek Kidner, *Ezra and Nehemiah: An Introduction and Commentary*, Tyndale Old Testament Commentaries 12 (Downers Grove, IL: InterVarsity, 1979), 71.
26. Mervin Breneman, *Ezra, Nehemiah, Esther*, New American Commentary 10 (Nashville: Broadman & Holman, 1993), 129–30.
27. Jason Meyer, *Preaching: A Biblical Theology* (Wheaton: Crossway, 2013), 249.
28. Jim Shaddix, *The Passion Driven Sermon* (Nashville: B&H, 2003), 126.
29. Jerry Vines and Jim Shaddix, *Power in the Pulpit*, rev. ed. (Chicago: Moody, 2017), 112.
30. The technical terms are "hermeneutics" (interpretation) and "exegesis" (study). For thorough discussions of the interpretation and exegetical processes, see Vines and Shaddix, *Power in the Pulpit*; Howard G. Hendricks and William D. Hendricks, *Living by the Book* (Chicago: Moody, 2007); J. Scott Duvall and J. Daniel Hays, *Grasping God's Word*, 3rd ed. (Grand Rapids: Zondervan, 2012); and Gordon D. Fee and Douglas Stuart, *How to Read the Bible for All Its Worth* (Grand Rapids: Zondervan, 1982).
31. John Knox, *The Integrity of Preaching* (Nashville: Abingdon, 1957), 89.
32. Millard J. Erickson, *Evangelical Interpretation: Perspectives on Hermeneutical Issues* (Grand Rapids: Baker, 1993), 54.
33. Albert Mohler, *He is Not Silent* (Chicago: Moody, 2008), 45.
34. D. A. Carson, *The Gospel According to John*, Pillar New Testament Commentary (Grand Rapids: Eerdmans, 1991), 534.
35. G. Abbot-Smith, *A Manual Greek Lexicon of the New Testament*, (Edinburgh: T & T Clark, 1950), 360.
36. William F. Arndt and F. Wilbur Gingrich, *A Greek-English Lexicon of the New Testament and Other Early Christian Literature* (Chicago,

IL: The University of Chicago Press, 1952), 669–70.
37. Arturo G. Azurdia, III, *Spirit Empowered Preaching* (Ross-Shire, Scotland: Christian Focus, 1998), 105. For further treatment of the Spirit's anointing in addition to Azurdia's work, see Vines and Shaddix, *Power in the Pulpit*, 76–77, 105–12.
38. Azurdia, *Spirit Empowered Preaching*, 109.
39. E. M. Bounds, *Power through Prayer* Grand Rapids: Baker, 1991), 69.
40. Ibid., 74.
41. John A. Broadus, *On the Preparation and Delivery of Sermons*, 4th ed., rev. Vernon L. Stanfield (San Francisco: Harper and Row, 1979), 10.
42. Ibid., 79.
43. Bryan Chapell, *Christ-Centered Preaching: Redeeming the Expository Sermon* (Grand Rapids: Baker, 2005), 33.
44. Lloyd M. Perry and John R. Strubhar, *Evangelistic Preaching* (Chicago: Moody, 1979), 73–74.
45. Donald Miller, *The Way to Biblical Preaching* (New York: Abingdon, 1957), 26.
46. Harold T. Bryson, *Expository Preaching* (Nashville: B & H, 1999), 9–10.
47. Chapell, *Christ-Centered Preaching*, 31.
48. Haddon W. Robinson, *Biblical Preaching: The Development and Delivery of Expository Messages* (Grand Rapids: Baker Book House, 1980), 18–19.
49. John A. Broadus, *A Treatise on the Preparation and Delivery of Sermons*, 2nd ed., rev. Edwin Charles Dargan (Nashville: Sunday School Board of the Southern Baptist Convention, 1897), 323.
50. George E. Sweazey, *Preaching the Good News* (Englewood Cliffs, NJ: Prentice-Hall, 1976), 42.
51. Tony Merida, *The Christ-Centered Expositor* (Nashville: B & H, 2016), 33.
52. Charles W. Koller, *Expository Preaching without Notes* (Grand

Rapids: Baker, 1962), 18–19.

53. D. Martyn Lloyd-Jones, *Preaching and Preachers* (Grand Rapids: Zondervan, 1971), 152–53.
54. Edwin Charles Dargan, *A History of Preaching*, vol. 1 (1905; repr., New York: Burt Franklin, 1968), 41.
55. Broadus, *On the Preparation and Delivery of Sermons*, 79–81.
56. Charles W. Koller, *Expository Preaching Without Notes* (Grand Rapids: Baker Book House, 1962), 72.
57. Robinson, *Biblical Preaching*, 37.
58. G. Campbell Morgan, *Preaching* (New York: Fleming H. Revell, 1937), 88.
59. Robert Smith, Jr. *Doctrine that Dances* (Nashville: B & H, 2008), 75.
60. Ibid., 76.
61. For additional information on sermon outlines, including examples of different kinds of developments, see Vines and Shaddix, *Power in the Pulpit*, 193–206.
62. Glen C. Knecht, "Sermon Structure and Flow," in *The Preacher and Preaching*, ed. Samuel T. Logan, Jr. (Grand Rapids: Baker, 1986), 276.
63. Broadus, *On the Preparation and Delivery of Sermons*, 109.
64. Brian L. Harbour, "Concluding the Sermon," in *Handbook of Contemporary Preaching*, ed. Michael Duduit (Nashville: Broadman, 1992), 221.
65. Broadus, *On the Preparation and Delivery of Sermons*, 113.
66. Harbour, "Concluding the Sermon," 221.
67. Vines and Shaddix, *Power in the Pulpit*, 217.
68. Bill Hull, *Right Thinking* (Colorado Springs: NavPress, 1985), 8.
69. Vines and Shaddix, *Power in the Pulpit*, 26.
70. Robert L. Thomas, "Exegesis and Expository Preaching," in *Rediscovering Expository Preaching*, ed. Richard L. Mayhue (Dallas: Word, 1992), 137.
71. Ibid., 143.

72. John R. W. Stott, *Your Mind Matters* (Downers Grove, IL: InterVarsity, 1972), 14.
73. Vines and Shaddix, *Power in the Pulpit*, 221.
74. H. C. Brown, *A Quest for Reformation in Preaching* (Nashville: Broadman, 1968), 64.
75. Vines and Shaddix, *Power in the Pulpit*, 223.
76. John A. Broadus, *On the Preparation and Delivery of Sermons*, 4th ed., re. Vernon L. Stanfield (San Francisco: Harper and Row, 1979), 168.
77. Ibid.
78. Ibid., 208.
79. Alexander Vinet, *Homiletics* (New York: Ivison, Blakeman, and Taylor, 1871), 177.
80. A. W. Tozer, *Of God and Men* (Harrisburg, PA: Christian Publications, 1960), 26–27.
81. Leon Morris, *The Epistle to the Romans*, Pillar New Testament Commentary (Grand Rapids, MI; Eerdmans, 1988), 436.
82. John R. W. Stott, *The Message of Romans: God's Good News for the World*, The Bible Speaks Today (Downers Grove, IL: InterVarsity, 2001), 324.
83. Thomas, "Exegesis and Expository Preaching," 138.
84. William D. Thompson, *Preaching Biblically: Exegesis and Interpretation* (Nashville: Abingdon, 1981), 10.
85. Al Fasol, *Essentials for Biblical Preaching* (Grand Rapids: Baker, 1989), 82.
86. George Edgar Sweazey, *Preaching the Good News* (Upper Saddle River, NJ: Prentice-Hall, 1976), 193.
87. William Evans, *How to Prepare Sermons and Gospel Addresses* (Chicago: Moody, 1964), 135.
88. Vines and Shaddix, *Power in the Pulpit*, 230–31.
89. Ibid.

90. Edgar M. Jackson, *A Psychology for Preaching* (Great Neck, NY: Channel, 1961), 162.
91. James D. Berkley, *Preaching to Convince* (Waco: Word, 1986), 91.
92. Jay E. Adams, "Sense Appeal and Storytelling," in *The Preacher and Preaching: Reviving the Art in the Twentieth Century*, ed. Samuel T. Logan, Jr. (Phillipsburg, NJ: P & R, 1986), 350.
93. Henry Grady Davis, *Design for Preaching* (Philadelphia: Muhlenberg Press, 1958), 158.
94. John MacArthur, Jr., "Moving from Exegesis to Exposition," in *Rediscovering Expository Preaching*, ed. Richard L. Mayhue (Dallas: Word, 1992), 294.
95. Broadus, *A Treatise on the Preparation and Delivery of Sermons*, 242.
96. E. Eugene Hall and James L. Heflin, Proclaim the Word! (Nashville: Broadman Press, 1985), 119.
97. Ralph L Lewis, *Persuasive Preaching Today* (Wilmore, KY: Asbury Theological Seminary, 1982), 210.
98. William H. Kooienga, *Elements of Style for Preaching* (Grand Rapids: Zondervan, 1989), 51--52.
99. John A. Broadus, *On the Preparation and Delivery of Sermons*, 4th ed., rev. Vernon L. Stanfield (San Francisco: Harper and Row, 1979), 210-11.
100. H. C. Brown, Jr., H. Gordon Clinard, and Jesse J. Northcutt, *Steps to the Sermon* (Nashville: Broadman, 1963), 156.
101. Merrill F. Unger, *Principles of Expository Preaching* (Grand Rapids: Zondervan, 1955), 18.
102. Clovis G. Chappell, *Anointed to Preach* (New York: Abingdon-Cokesbury, 1951), 25.
103. Michael A. G. Haykin, ed., *The Revived Puritan: The Spirituality of George Whitefield* (Ontario: Joshua Press, 2000), 35–37.
104. Elizabeth Achtemeier, *Creative Preaching: Finding the Words*

(Nashville: Abingdon, 1980), 92.
105. Lewis, *Persuasive Preaching Today*, 21.
106. Vines and Shaddix, *Power in the Pulpit*, 314.
107. Broadus, *A Treatise on the Preparation and Delivery of Sermons*, 252–53.
108. Achtemeier, *Creative Preaching*, 95.
109. Broadus, *On the Preparation and Delivery of Sermons*, 49.
110. Donald Miller, *The Way to Biblical Preaching* (New York: Abingdon, 1957), 114.
111. Andrew Blackwood, *Expository Preaching for Today* (Grand Rapids: Baker, 1943), 157.
112. Brown, Clinard, and Northcutt, 191.
113. Broadus, *On the Preparation and Delivery of Sermons*, 327.
114. Haddon W. Robinson, *Biblical Preaching: The Development and Delivery of Expository Messages* (Grand Rapids: Baker Book, 1980), 177.
115. Ibid., 187.
116. Andrew W. Blackwood, *Expository Preaching for Today* (Nashville: Abingdon, 1953), 153–54.
117. For fuller treatments—including biblical and theological grounds—of calling people to give expressions of response to the preached Word, see R. Alan Streett, *The Effective Invitation: A Practical Guide for the Pastor*, up. ed. (Grand Rapids: Kregel, 2004); Roy J. Fish, *Coming to Jesus: Giving a Good Invitation* (CreateSpace, 2016); Jerry Vines and Jim Shaddix, *Power in the Pulpit* (Chicago: Moody, 2017).
118. For a fuller discussion of these models, see Vines and Shaddix, *Power in the Pulpit*, 381–83.
119. For a fuller discussion of appealing to responders, see Vines and Shaddix, *Power in the Pulpit*, 383–85.
120. Jim Shaddix, "Is a Beeline the Best Line?" in Jerry Vines and Jim Shaddix, *Progress in the Pulpit* (Chicago: Moody, 2017), 124.

121. Ibid., 125.
122. David E. Garland, *2 Corinthians*, New American Commentary 29 (Nashville: B & H, 1999), 270.